Green Wickets

First published in 2007 by
Liberties Press
Guinness Enterprise Centre | Taylor's Lane | Dublin 8 | Ireland
www.LibertiesPress.com
General and sales enquiries: +353 (1) 415 1224 | peter@libertiespress.com
Editorial: +353 (1) 402 0805 | sean@libertiespress.com

Distributed in the United States by
Dufour Editions
PO Box 7 | Chester Springs | Pennsylvania | 19425

and in Australia by
James Bennett Pty Limited | InBooks
3 Narabang Way | Belrose NSW 2085

Liberties Press is a member of Clé,
the Irish Book Publishers' Association.

Trade enquiries to CMD Distribution
55a Spruce Avenue | Stillorgan Industrial Park | Blackrock | County Dublin
Tel: +353 (1) 294 2560 | Fax: +353 (1) 294 2564

ISBN: 978–1–905483–33–4

2 4 6 8 10 9 7 5 3 1

A CIP record for this title is available from the British Library.

Printed in Ireland by
ßetaprint | Bluebell Industrial Estate | Dublin 12

Green Wickets

LIB
ERT
IES

Ireland's Adventures at the **2007 Cricket World Cup**

Ed Leahy

Acknowledgements:

I went to the Caribbean to shoot some footage of the Irish cricket team playing at their maiden World Cup for a documentary on Irish cricket that I was developing with my friend Paul 'Ego' Keogh. I was also blogging my trip on the RTÉ website, www.rte.ie/sport/cricket/features/edsblog1.html. After the victory against Pakistan, I had to decide whether to stay on for an additional four weeks or to enjoy the last week in Jamaica and go home. As the trip was primarily a self-funded labour of love, the only issue stopping me from staying on was the state of my finances, so with a hefty available limit on my credit card and the generosity and support of several friends and family members, I bade Ego farewell and joined the caravan that was the Irish expedition at the 2007 Cricket World Cup.

Before departing Jamaica for Guyana, I gave my mate, and editor of DangerHere.com, Larry Ryan a call to see if there would be any interest back home in a book about one of the greatest Irish sports stories – which I was caught up in the middle of. Once home, I was introduced to literary agent Jonathan Williams, we had a meeting with Peter O'Connell and Seán O'Keeffe at Liberties Press, and a few days later the project was up and running. So a big thanks to Larry, Jonathan, Séan and Peter for bringing this book to life. The book is enhanced by some stunning photography, so a big thanks to Paul Mooney, Barry Chambers, Morgan Treacy and Inpho photography. And thanks also to the many cricket websites that I have trawled through over the past few months to check and double-check my notes and statistics from the 2007 Cricket World Cup, especially www.bbc.co.uk, www.guardian.co.uk, www.cricinfo.com and www.cricketeurope.net.

My passage through the Caribbean was made a lot easier thanks to the help and generosity of all the Digicel staff I encountered throughout the Caribbean, in particular David Hall and Maureen Rabbitt in Jamaica, Michael Kilcummins and Mia Fitzgerald in Guyana, and Patricia Maher in Grenada. I would also like to thank all the Irish media who travelled, in particular Paul 'Ego' Keogh, Emmet Riordan, Paul Davey, John Kenny, Ger Siggins, Robbie Irwin, Jerry O'Sullivan, Austin O'Callaghan, Neil Brittain, Albert Kirk and Richard Gillis.

Big thanks also to James Fitzgerald, Alison Mitchell, Martin Gough, David Courtney, the Ministry of Tourism in Guyana, Snoop Dogg from Hotel El Dorado, and Diamond, the best taxi driver in Jamaica. Respect!

I would like to say a huge thank you to my parents, Eddie and Bridget, my two brothers, Liam and John, my three sisters, Deirdre, Mary and Susan, and my girlfriend, Paula Hayes, for helping and supporting me immensely throughout this project. Thanks also to all my relatives and friends for all the encouragement, and to Tom Grealis and all the lads in the RTÉ Online sports department.

And a special thanks to Irish Cricket Union CEO Warren Deutrom, the ICU officials, and the entire Ireland travelling party, who were an absolute joy to be around in a personal and professional capacity throughout the journey. And to the men who made it all possible: Adrian Birrell, Trent Johnston, Kyle McCallan, Jeremy Bray, William Porterfield, Eoin Morgan, Niall O'Brien, André Botha, Kevin O'Brien, Andrew White, Dave Langford-Smith, Boyd Rankin, John Mooney, Paul Mooney, Peter Gillespie, Kenny Carroll, Roy Torrens, Matt Dwyer, Iain Knox, Peter Johnston and Phil Simmons. Thanks for the memories. It's all good.

Ed Leahy, November 2007

Contents

Foreword by Adrian Birrell   9

Introduction   10

1   The Road to the West Indies   17

2   Jamaica   23

3   Ireland v. Zimbabwe   33

4   Ireland v. Pakistan   45

5   Bob Woolmer   61

6   Ireland v. West Indies   69

7   Guyana   77

8   Ireland v. England   83

9   Ireland v. South Africa   95

10   Ireland v. New Zealand   105

11   Barbados   119

12   Ireland v. Australia   125

13   Ireland v. Bangladesh   133

14   Homeward Bound: Grenada   143

15   Ireland v. Sri Lanka   147

16   Adrian Birrell   159

17   Looking Back and Forward   165

Statistics   172

Picture credits
Picture credits Cover photo, Inpho; portraits on pp11–15, Paul Mooney; p16, Paul Mooney; pp18–19, Inpho; p22, Paul Mooney; pp24–25, Paul Mooney; pp28–29, Inpho; p30, Paul Mooney; pp34–35, Inpho; p38, Barry Chambers; p39, Inpho; p42, Inpho; p44, Paul Mooney; pp46–47, pp50–51, p52, p54, p56, Inpho; p58, Paul Mooney; pp62–63, Inpho; p66, Barry Chambers; p70, p74, p78, Inpho; p81, Paul Mooney; p84, p86, pp88–89, Inpho; p92, p94, p96, Paul Mooney; p98, Inpho; p102, Paul Mooney; pp106–107, p108, pp110–111, p112, Inpho; p114, p118, pp120–121, p124, Paul Mooney; p126, Inpho; p129, Paul Mooney; p130, Inpho; p132, Paul Mooney; p134, Inpho; pp136–137, p139, p142, p144, p146, p148, p150, pp152–153, Paul Mooney; p154–155, Inpho; p158, p163, p164, pp168–169, Paul Mooney.

Information on Inpho

Morgan Treacy has been a senior photographer with Inpho Sport Photography since 2002. Inpho was founded in 1988 by Billy Stickland and is Ireland's leading sports-photography agency. Morgan's work has brought him all over the world for Inpho but the Cricket World Cup in the West Indies was a unique experience.

'The Cricket World Cup proved to be an experience beyond all our expectations. From last-minute draws to world-beating heroes, with a murder mystery in between, Ireland's first involvement in a major cricket tournament truly was one of those moments that went beyond sport and gripped the nation. Getting to witness all this from a privileged position behind the camera was made all the more special by a squad of players and management who were open and enthusiastic and more than willing to share the highs and lows of their time in the Caribbean. The sense of being part of something never seen before is one rarely felt at major sports events these days, and that, along with the easygoing nature of the Irish and the West Indian people, made the 2007 Cricket World Cup an unforgettable experience for me.'

—Morgan Treacy

Inpho Sports Photography can be found at www.Inpho.ie

For my family and for Paula

Foreword

It gives me great pleasure to write the foreword for Ed Leahy's Green Wickets. The World Cup was an unforgettable experience: a perfect end for me personally to my five years with Irish cricket. Although I was at the helm during this period, the success cannot be attributed to one person but to a tremendous team effort. The fifteen players and four support staff put everything into the preparation, which culminated in the tie against Zimbabwe and wins against Pakistan and Bangladesh.

Preparation started many months before. The logistics of balancing work commitments with preparing properly for the biggest event in Irish cricket's history was a mammoth task in itself. Twelve out of the fifteen players were amateurs. The Irish Cricket Union delivered in this respect, and I was able to prepare the team as professionally as any other team in the competition.

The foundations were laid at our training camp in South Africa. The team ethic of 'no glory without hard work' was initiated here and continued throughout the campaign. This time in my home town was special for everyone but especially for me; in taking the players home to meet my family, the team became a 'family' too.

The Kenya campaign was very disappointing and hard to digest. In my view the preparation had been perfect, and in my experience good preparation always delivers results. Not so this time, however: sometimes you are not rewarded right away. Fortunately, we peaked at the right time and our efforts were rewarded in the World Cup proper.

Our fortunes started to change in Abu Dhabi. We beat the UAE inside three days, in a four-day fixture. This was a huge boost for the squad and meant that we set off for the Caribbean in good spirits.

The trip over there was an experience in itself. We were unaccustomed to such luxury. Business-class travel, liaison officers, security personnel, baggage masters and, best of all, police outriders. We were all in awe at how the other side of the cricket world lived, but we got used to it quickly too. Good performances against South Africa and Canada in our warm-up games sent us off to the group stages full of confidence. The self-belief required to do what we did had been nurtured and cultivated over a long period of time. We had learned through our successes as well as our failures. We knew that, on our day, we were a very dangerous side against any opposition and, most of all, we were not afraid to win.

This was proved with our performances against Zimbabwe, Pakistan and Bangladesh. These euphoric victories were offset by the sad and tragic loss of Bob Woolmer and our own Bob Kerr. These were difficult times, but I am proud that the team acted with dignity and respect.

Ed's book is an accurate account of the entire journey; the entertaining and witty script, as well as Paul Mooney's photos, provide the background and inside story – a story that I am very privileged to be part of, and which will remain in my memory forever.

Adrian Birrell, November 2007

Introduction

The Ireland squad that travelled to the World Cup was a motley crew of postmen, salesmen, electricians, farmers, schoolteachers and students – with the odd professional cricketer thrown in for good measure. With the exception of Niall O'Brien and Eoin Morgan, all of the players earned a living outside of cricket. Wicketkeeper O'Brien has played four years with Kent in English county cricket and signed a contract with Northamptonshire shortly before heading off to the Caribbean, while twenty-year-old Morgan joined Middlesex as a teenager and broke into the first team during the 2006 season. Fast bowler Boyd Rankin spent a few years in England with Middlesex and Derbyshire in between working on his family farm in Bready, near Strabane, County Tyrone. Rankin played under former England player and Ireland coach Mike Hendrick at Derbyshire and has since gone on to secure a professional contract with the club.

While others on the team have dabbled in English county cricket – Andrew White was at Northamptonshire for two years, and Kevin O'Brien and William Porterfield were over with Marylebone Cricket Club (MCC – the club that owns and is based at Lord's cricket ground in London) – the majority of the squad ply their trade in the Irish amateur cricket leagues. Captain Trent Johnston works as a fabric salesman, Kyle McCallan and Andrew White are PE teachers, John Mooney is an electrician, and Kenny Carroll works as a postman in Dublin. They generally play one game of cricket a week – weather permitting – and the only chance they have to be full-time cricketers is when they are away with the Ireland team.

The Ireland squad is made up of an almost-even mix of Leinster- and Ulster-born players, with the balance made up of the four who were born outside Ireland. And while it would be easy to assume that Trent Johnston, Dave Langford-Smith and Jeremy Bray from Australia, and André Botha from South Africa, were using the not-so-strict ICC laws to satisfy their personal ambitions to play at the World Cup, the reality of the situation tells a different story. Johnston first arrived in Ireland in 1995 as an overseas professional, returning home to play for North Sydney side Mosman during the Irish winter, and also represented New South Wales between 1998 and 2000. The all-rounder made his debut for Ireland in 2004 and soon established himself as captain.

Opening batsman Jeremy Bray is another Sydney-sider who starred for Australia at Under-19 level and would probably have got a senior cap if it hadn't been for the abundance of top players with whom he was competing. Justin Langer and Matthew Hayden – possibly the greatest opening partnership of all time – were just two of a crop of top-class batsmen in Australia while Bray was coming through. Bray also played for New South Wales and, like Johnston, started his career in Ireland as an overseas professional. Bray married an Irish girl, Geraldine, and has been living in Kilkenny for several years, where he works as a physical instructor. His first game for Ireland was in 2002, and he has been a regular in the team ever since.

David Langford-Smith, the opening bowler, arrived in Ireland for Bray's wedding and never went home. Langford-Smith plays for Dublin side Phoenix and made his competitive debut for Ireland in 2006. He lives in Dublin with his Irish wife, Maebh, and works for a garden-equipment company.

All-rounder André Botha first arrived in Ireland as a nineteen-year-old, again as an overseas professional. He couldn't speak much English when he arrived, but has long since settled in north Dublin, where he recently married his long-term Irish girlfriend, Yvonne. Botha qualified to play for Ireland in 2003 and rarely fails to impress with both bat and ball.

Ireland all-rounder Paul Mooney introduces the Irish squad that travelled to the 2007 Cricket World Cup:

JEREMY BRAY

Jeremy is an opening batsman who is great to watch in full flight. He moved to Ireland back in 1990s to play for Dublin side Phoenix. Since then, he has moved around and now plays his cricket for The Hills in Skerries. Jeremy was Ireland's opening batsman at the World Cup. In fact, the Sydney-sider has been a constant in the Ireland set-up since making his debut for his adopted country in 2002. His best score for Ireland is an impressive 190 against the UAE in 2005. Bray also plays as Ireland wicketkeeper when Niall O'Brien is away with his county side – or has acquired a suspension! Jeremy is also known as 'Wordsworth' – a nickname he picked up when he played in his first season of Grade 1 cricket in Sydney and talked the legs off his team-mates. Brayso's favourite pastimes are fines meetings and team functions, and his food of choice is frosty burgers.

WILLIAM PORTERFIELD

William is an opening batsman and also a superb fielder: Ireland's answer to Jonty Rhodes. He has had a brilliant start to his international career, scoring more than a thousand runs in his first full season. Porty has just signed a professional, two-year contract with Gloucestershire. He is also known as 'Wee Purdy' (to be pronounced with a north-western accent). He has played club cricket for Donemana but now plays for Rush when he is not busy with Gloucester. His favourite pastime is replacing bat grips.

EOIN MORGAN

A top-order batsman who holds the record score by any Irish batsman: 209 not out against the UAE at the Intercontinental Cup early in 2007. Eoin has always been destined for greatness and scored heavily as an underage player for club, school and country. He plays his cricket for Middlesex and had a good summer in 2007, hitting some high scores for his club. Eoin will score plenty of runs and break many more records in the future. Also known as 'Moggie', Eoin is best buddies with 'Wee Purdy', who also works tirelessly, and is now an expert bat-grip replacer too. His favourite pastime is sunbathing.

NIALL O'BRIEN

A batsman and wicketkeeper of high quality. Played some great innings during the World Cup and was fantastic with the gloves. Niall played at Kent as a professional for a number of years and is currently at Northants; he also plays for Railway Union, when available. He works extremely hard on his game and deserves all his success. He is capable of making a high score: his best is 176 against the UAE in 2005. Niall is very competitive and would be upset if he lost an egg-and-spoon race. His nicknames include 'Pebbles', 'Nipper' and 'Nobi', and his favourite pastimes include game drives and learning foreign dialects.

ANDRÉ BOTHA

A genuine all-rounder who can win a game with bat or ball. He first came to Ireland as a professional for Clontarf in the 1990s. After a few years to-ing and fro-ing to South Africa, he decided to stay, and he recently married an Irish girl. He now plays his club cricket for North County. In his first full year, André won the Irish Cricketer of the Year award. He qualified to play for Ireland in 2003 and has impressed with bat and ball ever since. His highest score for Ireland is 139 (against Herts) in 2003, and he took 4 for 23 (against ECB) the same year. André is also known as 'Chisel Chest', 'Rubber Jaw' and 'Raisins', and his favourite pastime is work.

ANDREW WHITE

An all-rounder who bowls off-spin and is a versatile batsman. Andrew came into the Irish set-up in 2000. He scored a hundred on his debut, against Denmark, and never looked back. He was a professional with Northants for two years and now plays club cricket for Instonians. Andrew works with Kyle, and lives next door to him too; they also have the occasional pyjama party. Andrew loves a practical joke, and he had his proudest day in Namibia when he and Kyle trashed two players' rooms in an unprovoked attack. Also known as 'Chalky', his favourite pastime is socialising with his team-mates.

KEVIN O'BRIEN

An excellent all-rounder who is a very effective and destructive batsman. He has played key roles with all the Irish underage teams. Kevin plays his club cricket for Railway Union. He is the younger brother of Niall, and the two are basically inseparable. They always enjoyed playing together in the touch rugby, and linked up well together! Also known as 'The Donk', Kevin's favourite pastimes include sunbathing with Moggie.

TRENT JOHNSTON

Trent is a fantastic all-rounder who has led the team superbly since his appointment in 2005. He captained Ireland to their first ever winner's medal in an international tournament, at the InterContinental Cup in 2005 in Namibia, two games after being named as captain. His best bowling came against Namibia last year, when he took 6 for 23. His highest score with the bat is 83, which he scored against Denmark in 2004. He now plays his cricket with Railway Union; I don't have enough time to go through his other clubs. Also known as 'Schmidt', his favourite pastimes include collecting poisonous spiders and taking the Pepsi challenge.

KYLE McCALLAN

Kyle is an off-spinning all-rounder who is Ireland's most-capped cricketer of all time. He is also the vice-captain of the current Ireland team and captained the side at the World Cup against the West Indies when Trent was injured. Kyle is a dedicated player and an inspiration to all young Irish cricketers. The Waringstown man began his cricketing career as an opening batsman before turning his attention to bowling. Kyle's best bowling came against Italy in 2000 (5 for 23); even more impressively, he once bowled Brian Lara for a duck in a NatWest Trophy game. He is always good value and loves a practical joke with his partner-in-crime, Andrew White. Also known as 'Queeny' and 'half-conversation McCallan', his favourite pastimes include free lunch interviews with AndrewWhite and holding four conversations at once.

BOYD RANKIN

Standing at 6 foot 8 inches, Boyd is Ireland's fastest bowler, regularly bowling at speeds in excess of 80 mph. He performed very well in the UAE with the Ireland A and Under-23s in 2006, and when he got his chance with the senior team, he took it. His best figures so far for Ireland are the 4 for 56 he took in the UAE in 2007. With his height, bounce and pace, he is very difficult to play when he gets things right. He has had an unfortunate season with his county side, Derbyshire: a broken leg kept him out of the team. Boyd was an iconic figure at the World Cup, and the people of the Caribbean really took to him: perhaps he reminds them of the bowlers of the great West Indies sides of the past. Nicknamed 'Stankin', his favourite pastimes include observing John Deere tractors.

DAVE LANGFORD-SMITH

An opening-bowling all-rounder who hits the ball a long way and scores some valuable late-order runs. He bowls beautiful out-swingers and is a handful on his day. In his first year in Ireland, 2001, he signed as a professional for Phoenix, and is now married to local girl Meabh. His best bowling for Ireland came against Scotland in the 2006 Intercontinental Cup, where he took 5 for 65. He comes from a place in Australia called Orange – where they grow apples – but is a full-blown Dub at this stage. His nickname is, imaginatively enough, 'Lanky', and his favourite pastime is doing Little Britain impersonations.

JOHN MOONEY

Another all-rounder who can be very effective in all three disciplines. John plays his club cricket at North County and has come up through the ranks with Niall O'Brien and Andrew White. John works very hard on his game and is one of the fittest members of the Irish squad. John took three wickets in Ireland's first official one-day international against England in 2006. He has been very patiently waiting for Liverpool to win a League title; hopefully they will do so before he becomes an OAP. Also known as 'Chadwick' or 'John Boy', his favourite pastimes are early-morning walks and the arts.

PAUL MOONEY

(introduced by younger brother John Mooney) After ten years' international service, Paul retired after the World Cup. The North County all-rounder has been a great servant to Ireland and will be missed both on and off the field. Paul's highest score for Ireland was 66 against Club Cricket Conference in 2003. He is a very placid man, known as 'Dog': his bark was always worse than his bite. Favourite pastimes include hanging out at the end-of-season umpires' party and placing orders for team food.

KENNY CARROLL

An opening batsman who had a brilliant season in 2006 and forced his way into the Ireland squad by scoring a huge number of runs, beginning in the UAE on an Ireland A tour. Kenny has a large appetite for work and always seems to be tucked away in a corner working on a specific area of his game or his fitness. He still needs to improve on his sprint training, though, after losing a contest against a member of the 'Oldies' while away on tour. Kenny loves the occasional stretch, and a stroll by himself to reflect on life. His nicknames are 'Squako', 'Heron', 'Plastic Bag' and 'Bundy'.

PETER GILLESPIE

Another player who retired from international cricket after the World Cup. Peter has been a great servant of Irish cricket since making his debut in 1995, and has proven to be a brilliant middle-order batsman who, incidentally, started his career as an opening bowler. Peter is a great character who is liked by all the squad and has scored many important runs for Ireland. His brother Mark also played for Ireland, winning four caps in the 1990s. The Strabane club man is one of an elite list to have more than a hundred international caps, and he holds the record for the quickest international century for Ireland, reaching the milestone in just forty-seven balls. Also known as 'Bubbsy' or 'Polish' as in 'shoe', his favourite food is shrimp.

ADRIAN BIRRELL

Adi is a cricket coach and tactician of the highest quality: his legacy is to have overseen the squad during the greatest period for cricket in Ireland. He very quickly gained the respect of cricket lovers throughout the county – a respect that he still commands. It was a pleasure for all of us to be part of his reign, and he will undoubtedly find success in whatever he decides to turn his hand to next. Adi's nickname is 'Benson', and his favourite pastimes are bird-watching and 'spotting' African game.

ROY TORRENS

Team manager and former Ireland international cricketer, Roy prefers to be called 'Robert' during fines meetings. Roy was the chief organiser at the World Cup; no job was too big or too small for him. He spent a great deal of time away from his bed-and-breakfast business in Portrush to travel with the team. He is a real character, and is also known as 'Fred Flintstone' – though I have no idea where that name came from! Roy's favourite pastimes include birdwatching, especially the all-too-elusive Famous Grouse.

IAIN KNOX

Physiotherapist and team shrink, Iain was a great person to have around, and was always willing to help out in any way, shape or form. He is a close friend and golf partner of Adrian Birrell, and they would always make time for a round wherever they went. According to Iain, he has never lost. Also known as 'Knoxy', his favourite pastimes include watching the misery of players as he ushers them into ice baths, and tearing bandage tape off their legs.

The team get a nice rest in business class en route to the Caribbean from London

1   The Road to the West Indies

On St Patrick's Day 2007, the Ireland cricket team caused one of the greatest shocks in cricketing history by beating Pakistan at the Cricket World Cup in the Caribbean. The result sent Pakistan out of the tournament and virtually guaranteed Ireland's qualification for the Super Eights, the second phase of the tournament. And while the win had the world's cricketing fraternity talking about Trent Johnston and his team of amateurs, it also prompted huge celebrations back in Ireland, the likes of which had only been seen with the football team in the glory days of Jack Charlton.

Ireland's World Cup journey had actually started back in July 2005 at the ICC (International Cricket Council) Trophy, where the top twelve Associate nations competed for the five remaining places at cricket's blue-riband event in the Caribbean. Ireland had lost to Scotland in the final, so they, along with beaten semi-finalists Canada and Bermuda, qualified automatically for the World Cup, with the Netherlands beating the United Arab Emirates in a play-off for the fifth and final place. As it turned out, Ireland arguably got a better draw than champions Scotland by being placed in Group D with the West Indies, Pakistan and Zimbabwe, while the Scots were in Group A with two of the favourites for the tournament, Australia and South Africa.

So with nearly two years to prepare for Ireland's first appearance at the World Cup, Adrian Birrell had plenty of time to think about the squad he would take. By the end of the 2006 season, the coach had made up his mind, and named the fifteen in September, in order to give the chosen players plenty of time to focus and for the squad to get to know each other ahead of their Caribbean sojourn. The squad trained throughout the winter at the North County Cricket Club in Balrothery, County Dublin, and in the New Year travelled to South Africa for hot-weather training ahead of the World Cricket League in Kenya at the end of January.

While in South Africa, the team spent eight nights of their three-week stay in Port Elizabeth with family and friends of Adrian Birrell, and played four competitive games against Eastern Provinces XIs ahead of the competitive games in Kenya and the Caribbean. Jeremy Bray was in top form with the bat, and Kenny Carroll, coming back from injury, hit a fine century as Ireland won two, lost one and tied one. They went into the World Cricket League showing some good form.

The trip to the coach's home town had the desired effect: the team gelled and got used to life – and each other – on the road as professional cricketers. In fact, the visit to South Africa was one of Birrell's fondest memories of the four months the squad spent together.

ADRIAN BIRRELL:

One of my highlights of the World Cup adventure was bringing the guys to see my home town, Port Elizabeth. It was very important for me to show them who I am and where I come from. I wanted the players to meet my friends and family, and that experience for me was just as memorable as the time we spent in the Caribbean.

After ideal preparations, and some well-earned results in South Africa, the team moved on to Kenya for the World Cricket League, which saw the five Associate nations compete with Kenya in a World Cup warm-up tournament. The competition gave the Irish players a chance to pit themselves against their fellow Associate nations in the World Cup format, the one-day game, and there was the added bonus of an invitation to the Twenty20 World Cup in South Africa in September 2007, with its very healthy prize fund of $250,000. The two finalists would qualify for the Twenty20 event; going into the tournament, Ireland fancied their chances.

The Nairobi event was a round-robin league format, with the top two teams contesting the final. First up for Ireland was Scotland; the Irish were beaten on the last ball of the innings, having set a target of 280 for Scotland. Ireland put their first, and only, points on the board in the next game, beating Bermuda, William Porterfield scoring an unbeaten 112 as Ireland won by four wickets. Then Kenya beat the Irish with

Sabina Park, Kingston, Jamaica, on St Patrick's Day

an over to spare, despite Ireland posting a decent total of 284, which included centuries from Porterfield and Kevin O'Brien. That result effectively ruled Ireland out of the final. To make matters worse, they lost to Canada and the Netherlands in their remaining games, to finish the tournament second from bottom.

Had Ireland won that tournament, the media interest in the World Cup might have been a bit more extensive, but newspaper editors, radio producers and television executives probably decided that it would be too risky to pump huge resources into the trip to the Caribbean. Fortunately, the results in Kenya seemed to spur on the Irish coach and players, who knew that they had let themselves down by not qualifying for the final and missing out on the Twenty20 event.

The Intercontinental Cup clash with the UAE couldn't have come at a better time for the Irish. Instead of returning home with their tails between their legs, the team went to Abu Dhabi knowing that victory would see them qualify for the final and help boost their confidence, and their exposure, ahead of the trip to the Caribbean. The game proved to be a resounding success for Adrian Birrell's charges, as they swept aside the opposition – and with it the painful memories of the Kenya tournament. On the field, records were broken, with Eoin Morgan recording the highest ever score for an Irishman as he hit 209 not out. Ireland won easily, by an innings and 170 runs, with a day to spare. The team, knowing that they had qualified for another final, could put the Kenya debacle behind them.

The squad arrived back from their African and Arabian expedition in mid-February. This gave them less than two weeks to spend at home before hitting the Caribbean. There was no time to relax: the players were in demand, fulfilling several engagements with their sponsors, Bank of Ireland, and attending a special reception at Áras an Uachtaráin to meet President Mary McAleese. The President welcomed the entire squad, their families and the Irish Cricket Union officials to a reception in the Phoenix Park, and she seemed genuinely enthusiastic about the team and their achievement as she chatted with the players over a cup of tea. The team looked resplendent in their official World Cup suits, as they were introduced individually to the President before posing for photographs for the media. The President revealed that her daughter plays cricket and that she and her family were looking forward to following the team's progress throughout the tournament.

Speaking at the reception, the players appeared to have put the bad results in Kenya behind them and were brimming with confidence ahead of their departure to the Caribbean.

TRENT JOHNSTON:

We'll be banking on beating Zimbabwe. We've beaten them before [at Stormont in 2003], so if we're on form and everyone plays to their potential, then there's no reason why we won't beat them. And we've beaten the West Indies before as well, two years ago in Belfast, but playing them in their own back yard is going to be difficult, with the home crowd behind them. And as for Pakistan, they could either hit us for 400 or we could roll them for 150. It really depends on which Pakistan team turns up on the day. They've also got a world-class bowling attack, so it will be very difficult to beat them. We'll just back ourselves and go out and enjoy it.

EOIN MORGAN:

The World Cup is a great opportunity for us to showcase the team as a group of talented cricketers. I think we have a huge chance of beating Zimbabwe, and then hopefully we can get a result against one of the better teams in the group. This would see us go through to play against all the top Test nations in the second phase.

While the team went away with few expectations from press or public – qualification was deemed a success and everything else a bonus – the coach had instilled a sense of belief in his team, knowing that anything was possible in one-day cricket. Birrell was quietly confident of surprising a few people in the West Indies.

ADRIAN BIRRELL:

I think we can beat Zimbabwe, even though they play a lot more cricket at a higher level than we do. We are definitely looking forward to that match. It's a big opportunity for us to win a match at the World Cup, and it would be fantastic to do that. We really want to win at least one game, and when we play the West Indies and Pakistan, they'll be the ones under pressure, as they have to win, which will allow us to go out and play with freedom in those two games. We look forward to being in that position.

The players also predicted that an upset was a distinct possibility.

NIALL O'BRIEN:

If you look back over the last few years since Adrian Birrell has been in charge, we've beaten two of the three teams in our group. Zimbabwe is the team we should beat, and then we're targeting the West Indies as well. Pakistan will be very difficult, especially if their two fast bowlers are back playing, but Zimbabwe and the West Indies are both definite targets.

The team arrived in Trinidad for two warm-up games ahead of the World Cup. First up was South Africa, which was a special game for Springbok Birrell. All-rounder André Botha would also compete against the country of his birth for the first time as an Irish cricketer. The game, at the Sir Frank Worrell Memorial Ground, was to lay down a marker for the Ireland team and what they would bring to the World Cup once the tournament started. The South Africans, the number-one-ranked side in the world, won the toss and decided to bat first, in order to use their allocated fifty overs; they probably thought that they wouldn't have needed their quota if they were to bat second.

Graeme Smith and his team of superstars got a rude awakening, as the Irish bowlers ripped into them from the start. Dave Langford-Smith couldn't have dreamed of a better haul, taking the wickets of A B de Villiers, Jacques Kallis and Graeme Smith for just thirty runs, only to be outdone by his skipper, Trent Johnston, who took 4 for 11 during his spell, leaving South Africa on 66 for 7. Andrew Hall came in with the Proteas in big trouble on 91 for 8 and hit a magnificent 67 to put a respectable score on the board. South Africa were finally all out for 192 off fifty overs.

Ireland came out chasing the very gettable target and looked comfortable with their task, at one stage needing only fifty-four runs with six wickets in hand, thanks to 37 from William Porterfield, 33 from Kevin O'Brien, and an impressive 40 from Botha. But then the tail collapsed, the last five batsmen scoring just six runs between them, and Ireland fell short by thirty-five runs. Beating a team as strong as South Africa would have been a huge achievement, but it seemed just as good to have been narrowly beaten, because it was only a warm-up game, and a win might have taken the team's eye off the bigger picture: the group games in Jamaica. This may have been one of the reasons why skipper Trent Johnston used eight bowlers, instead of bringing his openers back into the attack when the Proteas were struggling on 91 for 8.

TRENT JOHNSTON:

Where do you go after beating the best one-day team in the world? If we had won the game, that could have been our World Cup before it has even started. We would have had so much to live up to, and the pressure could have been too great. Now we still have Zimbabwe in our sights as a very winnable game, and an upset against Pakistan and the West Indies is definitely on.

The Ireland camp was growing in confidence, and the good vibrations were making their way back to the Emerald Isle, as the Blarney Army – assembling from all thirty-two counties and beyond – prepared to invade Jamaica for their premature summer holidays. Until that point, the only people who seemed to believe that the Ireland team were capable of a shock were Adrian Birrell and his squad, but now, after the performance against South Africa, Group D looked a lot more interesting, with Zimbabwe carrying no form into the tournament and Pakistan and the West Indies always liable to misfire.

The Ireland team went from strength to strength, three days later rolling Canada for 115. Langford-Smith again impressed with the ball, taking 4 for 41, with the opening batsmen easing past the target with more than 23 overs remaining, Jeremy Bray hitting 41 not out. This performance, against a team they had lost to in Kenya, showed that, in the proper conditions, Ireland were more than a match for any Associate nation. Jamaica beckoned.

Garlands at the ready as the team touched down in Trinidad for their first World Cup warm-up game

2 Jamaica

Bob Marley's birthplace was to became the adopted home for the Ireland cricket team at the 2007 Cricket World Cup, and Sabina Park in Kingston was chosen as the venue for all the games in Ireland's group, Group D. Jamaica is renowned as being the home of reggae music, the purveyor of Red Stripe beer, and one of the top holiday resorts in the world, boasting beautiful beaches across the island. And while the island's climate may be very different from Ireland's, there are many similarities between the two countries. Both nations used to be ruled by the English, tourism is a major source of revenue, and both have a history of mass emigration. In fact, there is a very strong Irish influence in Jamaica, as many Irish travelled to the Caribbean to work on the sugar plantations and set up home in places like Irish Town, Sligoville and Connaught. 'Murphy' is still a common surname in Jamaica, and there is also a great love for stout, with Guinness widely available throughout the island. Moreover, Jamaicans don't really care to pronounce their *ths* properly, and Gaelic words are commonly spoken as part of the Jamaican dialect, with *gansai* widely used as a name for a jumper. And many famous Jamaicans have Irish ancestry, including former Prime Minister Alex Bustamante, who used to describe himself as 50 percent Irish. The Jamaicans decided to rename the team 'Irie-land', 'Irie' being a local expression meaning 'everything is all right'.

The Ireland team arrived in Montego Bay on 9 March and spent the first few days relaxing at the Holiday Inn–Sunspree Resort hotel, from where they carried out all their officials engagements in the build-up to the tournament. Travel was kept to a minimum, as Jamaica was given the honour of hosting the World Cup Opening Ceremony, as well as the first game of the tournament, between hosts West Indies and Pakistan. The Irish team attended the Opening Ceremony on Sunday 11 March at the newly built Greenfield Stadium in the Trelawny district, on the north coast of Jamaica. The stadium was built specifically for the tournament and was one of several stadia funded by foreign nations: in this case, the Chinese government, under an agreement with the Jamaican government, funded the project to the tune of $30 million.

Arriving at the Opening Ceremony, the Irish team got the feeling that they had finally arrived on the world stage, as they rubbed shoulders with the world's elite in the players' enclosure, having spent most of the afternoon posing for the assembled media for the obligatory photocall. The team was paraded onto the playing field along with the other fifteen squads at the end of the spectacular event. The ceremony started slowly – very slowly – but gradually found its feet once the dignitaries and sponsors had said their piece. Traditional music representing all the competing teams followed, and the crowd started to find their voice as darkness fell and the lights came on. Even the area reserved for the teams, which earlier had looked quite uncomfortable, with the sun belting down, seemed to come to life, with some cricketers getting into the party mood and joining in.

The South African drummers provided the rhythm, and the Irish-dancing *cailíní* bounced onto the stage, ringlets flying, as they did the obligatory Riverdance-esque routine. Then the Duffys – not U2, as had been rumoured – provided more Irish music, which went down well with the locals, who naturally picked up the beat and clapped along enthusiastically. The local music was kept until the end; as you'd expect, it was fantastic. Every living Jamaican artist, old and new, seemed to show their face: Jimmy Cliff, Sean Paul, Shaggy, Buju Banton – they just kept coming.

The stadium was plunged into darkness for the final act, but this time it was a tribute. A beautiful homage to legend Bob Marley. Hit after hit was blasted around the stadium, with accompanying images of Marley in full flow back in his prime, as the I Threes did the backing singing live, in perfect harmony. If the tournament proved to be half as good as the music, it would be a World Cup to remember.

Irish captain Trent Johnston poses with the other fifteen captains on the beach in Montego Bay ahead of the Opening Ceremony in Jamaica

KINGSTON

The serious business began the next day, as the Irish team boarded a plane for the short flight to Kingston, where they checked into the now-infamous Pegasus Hotel to begin a two-week stay in the capital city. Also staying at the hotel were the other three teams in the group. Given that the hotel was in the centre of the city, the players were delighted with their surroundings and had plenty of options to help them pass the time that wasn't spent playing or training. The large outdoor swimming pool was well used, as were the in-house gym and tennis courts. The hotel is also situated close to the shopping district, and with several top restaurants to chose from, the Ireland team were spoilt for choice. Not that the team had too much time for relaxing or sightseeing. It was clear from the outset that they were taking the tournament seriously, and gruelling training sessions at the Kensington Park cricket ground and Sabina Park meant that much of the players' spare time was spent relaxing in their rooms or taking a post-training swimming-pool session with physio Iain Knox.

The cricket media were also omnipresent at the Pegasus, and a stroll through reception or one of the bars or restaurants would usually reveal a camera crew or journalist in deep conversation with one of the many superstars who were staying at the hotel. Despite the large media presence, players were left to go about their business in a calm and relaxed atmosphere. The Irish team in particular were very visible: they were clearly enjoying every moment of their World Cup adventure. Unfortunately, this all changed after the death of Bob Woolmer, when the hotel was overrun by the world's story-hungry news reporters.

For all its bad press about being the 'murder capital of the world', Kingston was a great place to be throughout the fortnight of the group stages. The city's nightlife is electric, and there wasn't a hint of trouble as cricket fans mingled with the locals in the bars, restaurants and nightclubs of the city centre. The locals pointed visitors in the right direction: Red Bones Jazz & Blues café in the city, and Strawberry Hills up in the Blue Mountains, were two of the best spots.

The main attraction in Kingston for the players, media and travelling cricket fans was of course the famous Sabina Park stadium, which has hosted top-class Test cricket since the 1930s and was the place where West Indies legend Garfield Sobers hit an unbeaten 365 – a world record that stood for more than thirty-five years. The stadium was renovated for the tournament to increase the capacity to 21,000.

THE BLARNEY ARMY

Thousands of Irish were exiled to the Caribbean in the 1600s by Oliver Cromwell, but in March 2007 it was a pilgrimage of choice, as two thousand Irish descended on Jamaica to support Ireland at the Cricket World Cup. And while Jamaica was boosted by the fact that the West Indies team was based in Kingston – guaranteeing big crowds and plenty of media exposure for the early stages of the World Cup – the country received another unexpected boost with the influx of the Irish supporters. In fact, Ireland was by far the best-supported Associate team and, as it turned out, one of the best-supported teams in the entire tournament after the hosts, the English and the Australians. Sure enough, the Blarney Army and the chilled-out island were a match made in heaven.

If you were lucky enough to be a member of the Ireland squad, you would have had no problems arriving in Kingston, as your bags would have been diverted automatically, your passport would have been stamped in advance, and a police escort would have transported you to your hotel within minutes of the plane touching down at Norman Manley Airport. The Irish fans weren't afforded that luxury, though, and had a bit of a trek before they could relax at their hotel of choice. And for the unlucky few who didn't have a lift waiting to pick them up, their first experience in Jamaica involved haggling for a taxi or minibus to take them on the cross-country joyride that is the two-hour journey to Ocho Rios. Most of the Irish fans were going straight to the resort town on the other side of the island, which meant a sixty-mile trip straight after the ten-hour flight from London or Dublin. And if there was no friendly face to greet you at the airport, there were plenty of willing locals in an assortment of vehicles ready to take you, your luggage and your money – American dollars, if you don't mind – to whatever point on the island you desired.

The journey from Kingston to Ocho Rios is a bit like a trip to the dentist to get a tooth filled. The first twenty miles to Spanish Town are like the waiting room: it's bearable, but you can't sit still thinking about the ordeal that awaits you. The mountains are like the dentist's chair. You really don't want to be there, but you know that it's a necessary evil. And the final descent from Fern Gully in to 'Ochi', as the locals call it, is akin to the horrible numb feeling you're left with as you leave: you're beyond caring, and all you're thinking about is getting home and finally spitting out all those last remnants of filling that seem to find their way into every part of your mouth. It really is a horrible journey, and is not the greatest introduction to a country that the rest of the world thinks moves in slow motion. In fact, the only good thing about going straight to Ocho Rios from the airport is that it is usually dark when you land in Jamaica, and you can't see how bad the roads that you are travelling on really are. And, of course, you wake up the next morning in the luxury of your Jamaican hotel room – provided that you haven't gone for one of the youth hostel-type dwellings that stand alongside the five-star alternatives.

Ocho Rios was the temporary home of the family and friends of the team, the members of the various cricket clubs from the north and south of Ireland, the Johnny-come-lately cricket fans, the Irish media – the hotels in Kingston were too pricey even for most of Ireland's media tycoons – and the rest of the bandwagon-jumpers.

The choice of hotels in Ocho Rios ranged from the $20-a-night basic room to the $500-a-night five-star luxury resort. The small hotels on the main street in Ochi housed many of the Irish, with the majority staying in the impressive Jamaica Grande Hotel, an all-inclusive beast of a hotel sitting pretty – that is, apart from the choice of paint colour, canary yellow – on the seafront adjacent to the harbour. There are, evidently, many nicer resorts on the island, and the beach at Ocho Rios is far from spectacular, but as two-week package deals go, you were well catered for. The hotel had several pools, a gym, tennis courts, games rooms, and various bars and restaurants. And as it was an all-inclusive resort, guests didn't have to pay a penny for as much food and drink as they could handle. This was the type of hotel facility that the Irish fans considered a challenge,

and revellers could be found propping up the bar as soon as the breakfast service was over.

Those unlucky enough not to be staying at one of the all-inclusive hotels – or lucky enough, as some might say – had plenty to occupy them throughout their stay in Ochi, and the World Cup coincided with Spring Break in the USA, which led to an influx of rowdy college types to add to the nightlife.

With only three days dedicated to cricket, there was plenty of spare time to travel around the island and view some of the sights, as most of the Blarney Army were there for a two-week break. Some of the tourist attractions within reach of Ocho Rios include the Dunn's River Falls, Nine Mile (where Bob Marley grew up) and the beaches of Port Antonio, some of which were used as locations for the film *Blue Lagoon*. The dedicated cricket fans braved the road to Kingston for the other group games which didn't involve Ireland, while just as many were happy to chill by the pool and enjoy the time off.

PETER GILLESPIE:

All I had heard about Jamaica before we came over was that it was the murder capital of the world, but since we arrived it has been amazing. We spent a few days in Montego Bay and met all our family and friends in Ocho Rios, and [the place] has really surprised me. The Jamaica that I have seen and the Jamaican people that I have met have been so friendly towards us.

DIGICEL

The Irish team had a ready-made fan club waiting for them on their arrival in the Caribbean. The Irish-owned mobile-phone company Digicel are a major player in Jamaica, with more than 75 percent of the market, having only set up in the country in 2001. Digicel is the largest Irish company operating outside Ireland and employs more than three hundred Irish staff throughout the Caribbean. They also sponsor the West Indies cricket team. Owner Denis O'Brien wanted to give the Irish team and supporters a proper *céad míle fáilte* when they arrived in Jamaica. As the World Cup coincided with St Patrick's Day, Digicel staff from all over the Caribbean descended on Kingston to celebrate the feast day and cheer on the boys in green.

David Hall, Oliver Chatten, Rachel Hehir, Liz Sheehan and Colman Clifford of Digicel amongst the Blarney Army in the Party Stand of Sabina Park enjoying St Patrick's Day

John Mooney has time to sit with family and friends at Sabina Park for a photograph

The Irish Cricket Union got their first taste of Digicel's generosity before the tournament began, when Digicel bought a shipment of jerseys for their staff in the Caribbean, with profits going towards the team's travel expenses. On arrival in Kingston, the Digicel crew brought the Irish team and media out to dinner at one of Jamaica's finest restaurants and promised all the players, management and media free credit for their mobile phones for the duration of the tournament.

3 Ireland v. Zimbabwe

Eighteen months after qualifying for the World Cup, the day of reckoning finally arrived: Ireland played Zimbabwe on 15 March 2007 at Sabina Park in Kingston, Jamaica. This was the group game that Ireland had targeted for victory, as Zimbabwe were struggling in the build-up to the World Cup, both on and off the pitch. Although Zimbabwe are full members of the ICC, they haven't played a Test match since 2004, and with the ongoing political issues in the country still unresolved, they have been unable to return to the Test scene. Both Australia and the West Indies cancelled planned tours to Zimbabwe in 2007 due to their governments prohibiting the tours.

Zimbabwe had qualified for the second phase of the previous two World Cups, but their form in the build-up to the 2007 tournament was poor. The Africans had been on the wrong end of a 5–0 series scoreline to Bangladesh and had actually lost fifteen of their last sixteen one-day matches. The international team had been in steep decline during the four years since Andy Flower and Henry Olonga had worn black armbands on 10 February 2003 in a World Cup match against Namibia in Harare. The players bowed out of international cricket after the tournament and were followed by several more top players, who no longer wanted to represent their country due to the political and social conditions in Zimbabwe.

Ireland went into the game full of confidence after a successful build-up in Trinidad, where they easily rolled Canada and came very close to beating South Africa. Adrian Birrell's side had beaten Zimbabwe at Stormont in 2003 by ten wickets, and that result, combined with Zimbabwe's recent form, gave Ireland confidence that they could repeat the feat at the World Cup.

TRENT JOHNSTON:
We'll be banking on beating Zimbabwe because we've beaten them before and they're not playing great at the moment: they were just beaten 5–0 by Bangladesh. So if we're on form and everyone plays to their potential, then there's no reason why we won't beat them. We are entering this match against Zimbabwe with a lot of confidence. We know we have a very tough group, but we have our plans in place, and we are looking to execute them. If a bit of luck goes our way, and we execute our plans, I believe we can make it to the next round.

Ireland went into the game with no injury worries, and Birrell was able to name his strongest team. He went with three opening batsmen: Jeremy Bray and William Porterfield as the preferred opening partnership, and Eoin Morgan at number three. Niall O'Brien, the wicketkeeping batsman, came in at number four, followed by all-rounders André Botha, Kevin O'Brien, Andrew White and Trent Johnston. Off-spinner Kyle McCallan would bat at nine, with the two fast bowlers, David Langford-Smith and Boyd Rankin, batting at ten and eleven. John Mooney was named as twelfth man for the opening game.

It was still dark at 5.30 am, when most Ireland fans set out from Ocho Rios for the game in Kingston. The journey was a helter-skelter road trip through the heartlands of Jamaica, followed by a taste of the early-morning rush-hour traffic in Kingston. Anyone who had left after 6 am would have done well to have been in their seats before the first delivery – at 9.30 am sharp. As the locals say, the two things that will always run on time in Jamaica are the church services and the cricket. Other Irish fans were flying up from Montego Bay; very few were staying in Kingston, as hotel prices had been hiked up for the duration of the tournament.

Once you made it to the vicinity of the stadium, you had to take a shuttle bus to the gates, where you and your belongings got a

Jeremy Bray enjoying the moment after hitting a magnificent century in Ireland's World Cup opener

thorough going-over before you were allowed to proceed to the magnificent Sabina Park. The press had it slightly easier, with organised transport from most of the big hotels to just outside the ground. Most of the Irish press travelled up from Ocho Rios on the morning of the game – which meant very early departure times to try to get to the Pegasus Hotel before the Irish team departed, in the hope of catching a word with one of the players or a bit of team news from the management.

The press box contained a sizable number of Irish journalists, when you consider that you'd get no more than a handful at an international match in Stormont or Clontarf. Most journalists were there an hour before the game commenced, and the mood was upbeat as they set their stalls out for Ireland's first-ever World Cup fixture. While the majority were hard at work, setting up laptops, organising ISDN lines, and the like, there were just as many sitting back doing nothing except chewing the fat – the lucky ones who were on a junket. Most had been through the accreditation process at the Opening Ceremony or the West Indies v. Pakistan game two days earlier, but those who had to go through the manoeuvres that morning were trawling through their goody-bags to see what freebies were on offer. For the record, the goody-bag contained a canvas World Cup laptop bag, a couple of guidebooks to the stadia and the players, a miniature fan complete with two AA batteries, and a bizarre set of DIY binoculars, which lasted about as long as the first bottle of complimentary water.

The press area itself was fantastic. The view was first class: behind the wicket on the first tier of the newly built Northern Stand. Square of the wicket, to the right of the Northern Stand, was the Kingston Cricket Club pavilion, an old-style colonial building that was starting to fill up ahead of the day's play, while adjacent was the George Headley Stand, which was far from full, but contained pockets of Irish fans throughout. Apparently, the old view from the Headley Stand was a sight to behold, with the spectacular Blue Mountains sprawling away from the city, and Kingston Harbour visible to the south. The view is still there, but unfortunately you have to go to the Northern Stand exits to see it.

The Irish players were out in the field going through a rigorous warm-up routine, while skipper Trent Johnston made his way into the middle for the toss. Zimbabwe captain Prosper Utseya called it right, and decided to bowl in the overcast conditions. Going into the tournament, Ireland's strength seemed to be in their batting, so Johnston was probably hoping to bowl first and chase down the total. Now it was up to his top and middle order to post a respectable score and for the team to try to bowl Zimbabwe out.

While there were fewer than three thousand in the stadium, the 'Party Stand' was full, and in flying form, twenty minutes before a ball had been bowled. The Blarney Army had turned up, and they were in fine voice as the first rendition of 'Come on you boys in green' began. There were more than a thousand Irish supporters in the Party Stand, singing and dancing to whatever tunes were booming out over the tannoy.

Ireland's opening batsmen strode out onto the pitch: William Porterfield took the first delivery, with Jeremy Bray at the non-striker's end. Christopher Mpofu opened with the new ball. So began Ireland's maiden World Cup encounter. The unfortunate statistic of 'first man out' came a bit too soon for Ireland's, and especially William Porterfield's, liking, as the left-handed Ulsterman edged the final delivery of the over to wicketkeeper Brendan Taylor. Taylor parried to second slip Vusimuzi Sibanda, who did well to hold on. Porterfield was out for a duck.

Eoin Morgan arrived at the crease a bit earlier than he would have hoped but at least he didn't have to face the next ball: the wicket ball had been the final delivery of the over. Bray prepared for his first delivery from new bowler Edward Rainsford and survived a big lbw shout with the opening delivery, before settling down to become Ireland's first batsman to score a run at the World Cup: the left-hander pushed into the offside for two runs. Morgan got off the mark in the fourth over, playing a straight drive for two as Ireland finished that over with six runs on the board. The fifth over saw Ireland's first boundary, as Bray made a beautiful cut for four, followed by the first six, again Bray cutting over point, to move Ireland onto a respectable 17 after five overs. Morgan followed suit by hitting a few boundaries himself, as Ireland pushed on to 42 for 1 after eight overs.

A change of bowling in the ninth and tenth overs saw Elton Chigumbura and Gary Brent come in, and they disrupted the Irish straight away with a maiden and a wicket respectively. Morgan went for 21 after he edged Brent, to give Chigumbura a straightforward catch in the slips. Niall O'Brien arrived at number four, with Ireland on 43 for 2. The wicketkeeping batsman, one of Ireland's few professional cricketers, signed for Northamptonshire prior to the World Cup, having spent four years at Kent. The older of the two O'Brien brothers in the squad came into the tournament in poor batting form, and continued in the same vein, going for one after nibbling at a Chigumbura delivery in the eleventh over, to give keeper Taylor an easy take.

Bray survived another strong lbw shout in the twelfth over, as André Botha – Ireland's fifth left-hander – came in to try to build a decent partnership. They managed to reach Ireland's first milestone, with the scoreboard reaching 50, before Bray smashed another six as he settled into an impressive start to his World Cup campaign. Botha, on the other hand, hung around for only four overs, managing a solitary run from seven deliveries faced, before being bowled by Chigumbura. The all-rounder shouldered arms, misjudging the straight delivery, which smashed the top of middle stump. Ireland were in trouble, on 64 for 4 after fifteen overs.

Ireland's number six was right-handed batsman Kevin O'Brien, younger brother of wicketkeeper Niall, and he immediately went on the attack. He edged a Brent delivery for four, the ball flying just out of reach of the wicketkeeper, and quickly moved on to eight, while Bray survived a close run-out in the nineteenth over. At last, the Irish looked like they would put on a partnership, as Bray closed in on his, and Ireland's, first World Cup half-century. But the Railway Union man slashed at a Rainsford delivery and edged behind to Taylor. O'Brien was out for 10, to leave Ireland on 89 for 5 after twenty-two overs.

Former Northants off-spinner Andrew White, from Down, joined Bray in the middle. The opener brought up his fifty soon afterwards, off sixty-six deliveries. The Irish run rate slowed as Bray and White cautiously built a partnership. White pushed past twenty-five with some unorthodox shots, while Bray kept things moving at his end, bringing up a fifty partnership and taking the score to 145 after thirty-seven overs. Then White was bowled lbw by Brent in the thirty-eighth over, out for 28 off forty-eight deliveries, as captain Trent Johnston came in at number eight with twelve overs still remaining.

Johnston, a renowned quick scorer, found the pace almost immediately, and a decent partnership seemed to be building before the rain started to fall in the forty-third over. The players left the field with Bray thirteen short of his century. Play resumed twenty minutes later, but the break seemed to have distracted the captain. With eight runs already scored in the forty-fourth over, Johnston went after a single, but Bray sent him back, and the captain was run out after reaching 20 off twenty-four balls. Ireland were now 182 for 7; Kyle McCallan went for a duck in the following over as he played a slog-sweep and was stumped by Taylor, to make it 182 for 8. Fast bowler David Langford-Smith came in at number ten, and settled in remarkably quickly for a tail-ender, getting off the mark with a single, to give the strike back to Bray.

Bray completed his century in the forty-eighth over with a perfect square-drive off a Mpofu delivery, to reach 103 from 129 balls. The Party Stand celebrated with him as Bray enjoyed the moment in the middle. The entire Irish team were applauding from the balcony of the pavilion, as were the, predominately Irish, journalists in the press box. It was a remarkable achievement in Ireland's first taste of World Cup cricket. The total pushed past 200 in the same over and then Bray and Langford Smith let loose for the last twelve deliveries scoring a quick twenty before Langford Smith was out on the last ball, top-edging to Taylor off Mpofu's final delivery. Langford Smith finished on 15 from seventeen balls, while Bray was unbeaten on 115 from 139 deliveries, to give Ireland a respectable total of 221 for 9 off the fifty overs.

Players celebrate the end of the Zimbabwe game

Andrew White tries to run out Edward Rainsford in the final over against Zimbabwe

Lunch was taken. And while the choice between pork and jerk chicken was a difficult one, the more-important debate began as to whether Ireland's total was enough or whether they had fallen about twenty or thirty runs shy of a winning score. The West Indies had posted 241 to win two days previous at the same venue; they had then bowled Pakistan out for 187. The chances of Zimbabwe posting a score of more than 250 were therefore small, although a great deal still depended on the Irish bowling. The required run rate was just under 4.5 runs per over, so if Ireland kept the rate below five and were tight with their bowling at the death, they stood a very good chance of victory.

Langford-Smith bowled Ireland's first World Cup over to Terrence Duffin, who opened the Zimbabwe innings with Vusi Sibanda. Boyd Rankin shared the new ball with Langford-Smith, but it was Zimbabwe who looked more comfortable in the opening overs, as they reached 25 for 0 after five. Rankin's pace began to make inroads in the sixth over, as Duffin was dropped twice, first by keeper O'Brien and then by Morgan at second slip. The batsman could hardly contain himself as he rode his luck: he was laughing at his crease as Rankin fumed, walking back for the final ball of the over. The fast bowler had found his line and length and was giving the batsman an awful time. But thankfully for Ireland – and just reward for Rankin – it was third time lucky: the last ball of the over was edged to O'Brien, who made no mistake, and gave Ireland their first victim of the World Cup. Rankin celebrated, but still had time to glare at Duffin, who made his way back to the pavilion as the Irish fielders swarmed around the man from Bready.

Zimbabwe maintained their strong run rate as they reached fifty after ten overs, with Sibanda already on 33. The next ten overs saw a change in bowling, with Johnston and Botha slowing down the rate, but Sibanda pushed past his fifty, and at 87 for 1, Zimbabwe were in command. Then, in the twenty-first over, Johnston struck, as Justice Chibhabha played a poor shot and Langford-Smith took an easy catch, the Zimbabwe number three out for twelve. Sean Williams was next in for Zimbabwe. Williams had impressed in the World Cup warm-up games, scoring 72 against Canada and a very respectable 44 in the Australia fixture, and he had already bowled six tight overs earlier on, taking McCallan for a duck with his left-arm spin. Williams went after the Irish bowlers, and Zimbabwe pushed past 100. McCallan came into the attack seeking retribution for his earlier stumping, and Williams made it easy for the Warringstown man as he danced down the wicket and lobbed a poor shot to Rankin. Williams was out for 14, to leave Zimbabwe on 107 for 3. Ireland were back in the game.

Andrew White came into the attack as Johnston decided to go with a spinner at either end in an attempt to dislodge Sibanda. However, it was the new man in, Stuart Matsikenyeri, who started to wreak havoc. After surviving a near run-out on his first delivery, he hit some awesome shots, and moved on to 15. Zimbabwe were cruising, on 129 for 3. Just when it looked as though the Irish attack had run out of ideas when it came to getting Sibanda out, the opener trod on his stumps, and departed on 67. In the next over, Elton Chigumbura went for four, thanks to a great catch from batting hero Jeremy Bray off Johnston's delivery. So now Zimbabwe were sitting on 133 for 5 with twenty overs remaining. That left them requiring eighty-nine runs at a run rate of just over four. With Matsikenyeri the only recognised batsman remaining, the game had swung back in Ireland's favour.

The morning cloud had been replaced by afternoon sunshine, as Ireland went about cleaning up the tail. But again the game swung back in favour of Zimbabwe, as they scored fluently off the next twelve overs. Johnston had brought Rankin and Langford-Smith back into the attack, but to no avail. Johnston then came back on himself and, as the final throw of the dice, put Kevin O'Brien on to bowl. O'Brien was hit for eight off the over. This surely spelt the end for Ireland: Matsikenyeri pushed past fifty – thanks to a dropped catch on the boundary from centurion Bray – as Zimbabwe reached 198 for 5. The Africans needed just twenty-four runs from forty-two balls, with plenty of wickets to spare.

In the forty-fourth over, Ireland were given a lifeline as Brendan Taylor was run out thanks to a bit of ingenuity – or plain old luck – from McCallan. With Taylor out of his ground, McCallan deflected a fierce drive on to the non-striker's stumps. Considering that he had his back to the stumps, only McCallan could tell you if he meant it or not. Significantly, the run-out broke an impressive partnership that had reached 70 from eighty-one balls.

Taylor's run-out put the brakes on Zimbabwe's free scoring, as only five runs were scored in the next three overs. Johnston finished his overs with very respectable figures of 10–2–32–1. Botha followed in the next over, to post identical figures to Johnston. He took the wicket of Brent in the process, the experienced Zimbabwean out lbw for three. Zimbabwe now needed nine from twelve deliveries, with three wickets in hand.

What happened over the next two overs will probably never be surpassed in terms of excitement, anxiety and emotion for anyone who was present in Sabina Park, whether Irish, Zimbabwean or neutral. Even trying to write about the final two overs brings back an experience that was, at the time, impossible to take in. Only after several viewings of the last twelve balls, courtesy of our good friends at YouTube, is it possible for me to comprehend what actually went on in Kingston that day.

Paresh Soni (BBC cricket commentator):
This is just the most awesome, spine-tingling atmosphere. Whatever the result, this is a great day in Irish cricketing history.

First of all, the skipper tossed the ball to O'Brien the younger when the experienced McCallan, Langford-Smith and Rankin still had overs to spare. O'Brien had recently turned twenty-three, and his only previous over had gone for eight runs. But sure enough, O'Brien repaid his captain's faith, bowling a double-wicket maiden. A full toss from the first delivery tempted Prosper Utseya, but he drove straight to extra cover, into the hands of Morgan, prompting O'Brien's one-legged dance celebration. A couple of dot balls and a bit of fancy footwork later, and new batsman Mpofu, trying to get Matsikenyeri back on strike, ran himself out, Johnston hitting the stumps with a direct hit. In fact, he would have had time to walk to the wicket with the ball, Mpofu was so far out of his ground.

This left Zimbabwe needing nine to win off the final over, with the Irish knowing that one more wicket would secure victory.

This time Johnston went to Andrew White to bowl the final over. White had only bowled two overs but had already taken a wicket, and Johnston was confident that he could deliver. Coach Matt Dwyer, coach in waiting Phil Simmons, and team manager Roy Torrens were looking very anxious on the balcony, but Adrian Birrell was nowhere to be seen. He was probably pacing up and down the dressing-room area: he is the first to admit that he is a terrible watcher of cricket. The first three deliveries yielded five runs, leaving Zimbabwe needing four to win from three deliveries. New batsman Edward Rainsford was now on strike, and he squeezed one through the gap to put Matsikenyeri back on strike with two balls remaining. The batsman went after the next ball, slicing it high over backward point. Johnston almost made the catch of his career but couldn't hold on to the ball. Zimbabwe ran two, and tied the score with one ball remaining.

Sabina Park was buzzing as Johnston brought the field right in to try to save the single. White's delivery was missed by Matsikenyeri, and Niall O'Brien caught the ball and removed the bails. He then realised that Rainsford was outside his crease, so he lobbed the ball to the far end to run out the non-striker. Huge confusion followed as to what had happened, but it didn't matter: Ireland had tied. The players celebrated as if they had won the game. Only when normality was restored did it become clear that Zimbabwe had been bowled out, but a tie was the result as the score was level. Rumours had started that Ireland had won as they had a man spare. Was this a new rule for the World Cup? Nobody knew, and it made no difference anyway: the fact that Ireland had not been beaten in their first-ever World Cup encounter was something to celebrate.

Kyle McCallan:
The run-out was definitely a major turning-point in the game, although I can't say for certain that I can take full responsibility for it. Adi [Birrell] is always at me to improve my fielding off my own bowling so maybe it was a blessing in disguise that my fielding was not perfect, otherwise I may have stopped the ball. Having said that, it's an area I've worked very hard on so there's always a chance that you'll get the run out when you manage to deflect the ball on to the stumps, which is what happened in this instance.

One of the tournament's best fielders, William Porterfield gets ready to pounce versus Zimbabwe. Meanwhile, former Irish Times journalist, James Fitzgerald [white shirt in background], who now works for the ICC in Dubai, takes a break to catch a bit of the action

ANDREW WHITE:

Once I heard I was going to bowl the last over, I just got my mind ready to bowl it. So before the over, I wasn't too bad, but then I sensed some of the crowd's reactions and emotions as the over went on. I'd planned where I wanted to put each of the balls before I bowled it, but it never materialised that way. The ball never actually went where I wanted it to go. But looking back, maybe that wasn't a bad thing, as the batsman wasn't able to read what I was going to do, and I think that paid off in the end. It's not something I would like to do too often. It's nice to come out on the good side of it, but having experienced a couple of near misses in Kenya, it was nice to come out on top on that one.

The team did a lap of honour to pay respect to the awesome support they had received from the Blarney Army and the locals, who had turned out to watch a good game of cricket and had been well entertained. Jeremy Bray was named man of the match and received his accolade as he was being interviewed pitchside, with his team-mates looking on and applauding. The result left Ireland and Zimbabwe tied for second behind the West Indies, with Pakistan propping up the table with no points. Next for Ireland was a return to Sabina Park two days later for a St Patrick's Day fixture with the mighty Pakistan. Surely it couldn't get more exciting than this?

Ireland v. Zimbabwe   Umpires: I G Gould, B G Jerling

Ireland innings			runs	balls	4s	6s
W T S Porterfield	c V Siband a	b C B Mpofu	0	6	0	0
J P Bray	not out		115	139	10	2
E J G Morgan	c E Chigumbura	b G B Brent	21	27	4	0
N J O'Brien	c B R M Taylor	b E Chigumbura	1	5	0	0
A C Botha		b E Chigumbura	1	7	0	0
K J O'Brien	c B R M Taylor	b E C Rainsford	10	28	2	0
A R White	lbw	b G B Brent	28	48	3	0
D T Johnston	run out		20	24	2	0
W K McCallan	st B R M Taylor	b S C Williams	0	3	0	0
D Langford-Smith	c B R M Taylor	b C B Mpofu	15	17	1	0
Extras		3nb 5w 1b 1lb	10			
Total		for 9	221		(50.0 ovs)	

Bowler	O	M	R	W	Fall of wicket	
C B Mpofu	10.0	3	58	2	0	W T S Porterfield
E C Rainsford	7.0	0	44	1	43	E J G Morgan
E Chigumbura	6.0	2	21	2	44	N J O'Brien
G B Brent	10.0	1	40	2	64	A C Botha
P Utseya	10.0	0	29	0	89	K J O'Brien
S C Williams	6.0	1	21	1	145	A R White
S Matsikenyeri	1.0	0	6	0	182	D T Johnston
					182	W K McCallan
					221	D Langford-Smith

Zimbabwe innings			runs	balls	4s	6s
T Duffin	c N J O'Brien	b W B Rankin	12	22	2	0
V Sibanda	hit wicket	b A R White	67	84	9	0
C J Chibhabha	c D Langford-Smith	b D T Johnston	12	36	1	0
S C Williams	c W B Rankin	b W K McCallan	14	13	2	0
S Matsikenyeri	not out		73	77	9	1
E Chigumbura	c J P Bray	b W K McCallan	4	9	0	0
B R M Taylor	run out		24	40	3	0
G B Brent	lbw	b A C Botha	3	12	0	0
P Utseya	c E J G Morgan	b K J O'Brien	1	3	0	0
C B Mpofu	run out		0	5	0	0
E C Rainsford	run out		1	1	0	0
Extras		2nb 7w 1lb	10			
Total		all out	221		(50.0 ovs)	

Bowler	O	M	R	W	Fall of wicket	
D Langford-Smith	9.0	0	34	0	26	T Duffin
W B Rankin	7.0	1	43	1	92	C J Chibhabha
A C Botha	10.0	2	32	1	107	S C Williams
D T Johnston	10.0	2	32	1	128	V Sibanda
W K McCallan	9.0	1	56	2	133	E Chigumbura
A R White	3.0	1	15	1	203	B R M Taylor
K J O'Brien	2.0	1	8	1	212	G B Brent
					213	P Utseya
					213	C B Mpofu
					221	E C Rainsford

4 Ireland v. Pakistan

St Patrick's Day is celebrated in every city, town and village throughout the world that has an Irish connection – and in many more that have no links with Ireland but like to celebrate the day anyway. Kingston was getting an extra-special party this year, as the feast day coincided with Ireland's second game in the World Cup. Pakistan – another side that wears green – were the opposition, and while they were well aware that the Irish were celebrating, the number-four-ranked team in the world were planning to make sure that the party remained in the stands and not on the pitch.

If there were 1,500 Irish fans for the Zimbabwe game, there were at least another 500 that had turned up for the clash with Pakistan. Irish people were flying in from all over the world to join up with the Blarney Army and sample the World Cup experience. A Gaelic-football team flew in from the Cayman Islands, ex-pats were jetting in from the USA, honeymooners were diverting flights from South America, and others who were travelling in the area made a point of turning up to support the boys in emerald green. A lot of the Blarney Army had been celebrating the feast day with the Kingstonians at the open-air venue Mas Camp the night before. Partygoers received a free St Patrick's Day plastic hat upon entry, even if the music wasn't necessarily of the Irish persuasion. Many of the hats had made it to the game at Sabina Park and were on show in the already full Party Stand.

At 9 am the match programme feed kicked in on the many televisions throughout Sabina Park. The introduction brought us pitchside, as usual, first for a look at the wicket, and then for the toss. And if the Jamaican tourist board was doing its best to ensure that the St Patrick's Day celebrations were in full swing on the terraces, the Sabina Park groundsmen were doing their utmost to join in the fun by producing one of the greenest wickets ever to be unveiled in the Caribbean.

Michael Holding was reporting on the condition of the pitch and was trying his best to keep a straight face when he analysed the grass-laden wicket. Part of the pitch was bare, and there were several small cracks close to where the batsman stands, but the rest of the pitch, especially where the ball would be pitching, was extremely green, with lots of grass on it. The ball would move off the grassy areas and make things difficult for the batsmen.

MICHAEL HOLDING:

If you move down the pitch a bit further, you will see a lot of grass all over the wicket. This is a lot of grass. We didn't see so much grass on the other two pitches that have been used. Not too sure as to whether it's because it's St Patrick's Day that they left all this greenery. Ireland should be happy with that. I'm not too sure how happy the batsmen will be when they see how much it moves off the seam. But the colour, certainly happy with that, Ireland.

Pakistan coach Bob Woolmer was also a bit apprehensive about the pitch, but he did his best not to criticise it, as he knew that his side was under pressure to win their two remaining games.

BOB WOOLMER:

Specifically after the tie [Ireland v. Zimbabwe] we now have to win both games to get through. We are quite aware of the situation, I can tell you. I know a lot of them [the Irish] in terms of my studying. I was at both their games in the warm-ups and I've been following their results carefully, hopefully as a coach should do. They carry about five or six lefthanders up front and they've got a useful bowling attack; specifically, if there's a bit of grass on the wicket, they hold their line pretty well. They're a useful side in terms of an Associate side, and are arguably the best Associate side here in the West Indies. It's a banana-skin-type fixture for us, but we are aware what we have to do. I know the ICC are looking for one of the Associate sides to beat one of the senior sides, and I just hope it's not us today.

The Irish team celebrate beating Pakistan in Sabina Park with a well-deserved lap of honour

Back in the studio with host Pommie Mbangwa were former West Indies wicketkeeper Jeffrey Dujon and one-time Pakistan batsman Aamir Sohail. Both had predicted Pakistan to win comfortably at the start of the broadcast but, after sensing Woolmer's cautious approach, and seeing the state of the pitch, they started to change their tune, saying that the wicket would suit Ireland and that Pakistan would have to take the game very seriously. They also agreed that the toss would be vital, as the pitch would definitely suit the bowlers.

The ground was starting to fill up, with at least one thousand more people in the stadium than had watched the Ireland v. Zimbabwe game. Pakistan had about the same number of people supporting them as Zimbabwe had had – no more than a hundred – so the extra thousand were probably made up of roughly half Ireland fans and half locals who were out to watch a good game of cricket. The weather was hot but cloudy and, with rain forecast for the afternoon, there were bound to be a few breaks in play. As well as the greenness of the wicket, the cloud cover would give the bowling side an advantage early in the game.

Trent Johnston and Pakistan captain Inzamam-ul-Haq were in the middle with match referee Chris Broad for the toss. It was first blood to the Irish, with Trent Johnston calling it right and deciding to bowl.

TRENT JOHNSTON:

It might swing a bit, and a bit of seam off the deck as well, so we're going to have a bowl. We're going to come out here and try and put a bit of pressure on the opening batsmen of Pakistan and see if we can get some early wickets. It's a fairy tale [to win on St Patrick's Day], but we're going to come out here and give it our best and try and be competitive. And if we can execute our plans and perform very well in our three disciplines, we're going to give them a fight.

Inzamam knew that the toss was vital, and it was obvious that he wasn't too happy to be going in first. He was still smiling, however, as he tried to play down the significance of the green wicket.

INZAMAM-UL-HAQ:

If you lose the toss, you're ready for this. The wicket is good for the fast bowlers, and batting is not easy, as the ball will not come on to the bat, but after twenty overs I think it is a good batting track. We have no option to take it easy today, as they performed very well in the last game. We'll be taking it very seriously and ensuring good cricket.

Adrian Birrell, unsurprisingly, had gone with the same side that had performed so well against Zimbabwe, although Pakistan made a couple of changes. Azhar Mahmood, the all-rounder, came in for Naved-ul-Hasan, and fast bowler Mohammad Sami replaced leg-spinner Danish Kaneria as a result of the condition of the pitch: the Pakistanis were opting for seam over spin, despite Ireland's inexperience against top-class spinners. The Pakistan line-up was still a who's who of world cricket. Woolmer's side had three of the finest batsmen in the world in the form of Younis Khan, Mohammad Yousuf and Inzamam-ul-Haq, although they were missing star bowlers Shoaib Akhtar and Mohammad Asif, who had been left out of the squad through injury.

The parade would have just been making its way down O'Connell Street in Dublin at about the same time that David Langford-Smith bowled the first ball in Sabina Park, but Jamaica was five hours behind the Irish capital, and by 9.30 am the festivities were well and truly up and running. Even the folk back home would have been impressed by how seriously the Jamaican Irish were taking the patron saint's day of celebration. The opening few balls were less impressive. With five deliveries remaining in the first over, Pakistan had already reached seven for no wicket, thanks to a single off the first ball, a wide and a no-ball boundary. Trent Johnston's prophecy that Pakistan were capable of scoring 400 suddenly looked realistic. Langford-Smith was having difficulty getting his approach right – he had pulled up before the opening delivery – and the wide and the no-ball put immediate pressure on him to do something with the new ball.

After the second delivery, Niall O'Brien ran thirty yards to have a word with Langford-Smith, apparently suggesting that he change his line and length, and bowl back of a length. The next three deliveries were dot balls, and then, off the last delivery of the over, Mohammad Hafeez clipped an outside edge that went straight to O'Brien behind the stumps. A wicket in the opening over was just what Ireland were looking for. Suddenly Sabina Park came to life, as Younis Khan walked out to join Imran Nazir in the middle.

Boyd Rankin shared the new ball, and it wasn't long before the big Bready man was making an impact on proceedings. In fact, his first delivery had Nazir on his knees after he took the full brunt of the new ball somewhere in the mid-region: Rankin meant business. His second over was even more productive: Rankin tempted Khan into playing the shot, and Khan obliged, edging to the slips, where André Botha took an easy catch. Once again, the combination of Pakistan's opening batsmen having problems, combined with the fact that they tend to struggle on a green wicket, reaped dividends for Ireland. Pakistan were on 15 for 2, Khan departing for a duck.

Next in for Pakistan was Mohammad Yousuf, widely regarded as the best batsman in the world going into the World Cup. Yousuf looked composed as he started to build a partnership with Nazir. Pakistan got through the opening powerplay without further loss, and posted a tidy 43 on the scoreboard. Captain Trent Johnston brought himself into the attack alongside André Botha; not for the first time, his decision was to bear fruit almost immediately. Yousuf, who had pushed on to 15 as Pakistan brought up their half-century, attempted to hammer a square drive but couldn't control the shot, and it flew to William Porterfield at backward-point. Yousuf looked on disbelievingly, before reluctantly turning and making his way back to the pavilion.

Captain Inzamam-ul-Haq entered with his side struggling on 56 for 3. Inzamam was playing in his fifth World Cup, and had more than 11,000 runs to his name in one-day internationals before the meeting with Ireland. He probably thought that he wouldn't get a chance to add to his tally against the Irish: on their day, his openers should have easily dealt with the Irish

attack. Now, though, it was up to him to put on a captain's performance and pull his side out of danger. But it was the Ireland captain who was making the right choices as his change of bowler, Botha, fired one in to Inzi. His tentative effort was edged behind, for Eoin Morgan to take an impressive catch low down at slip. The specialist right-hand batsman had been dismissed on his third ball for just one run. Pakistan were 58 for 4 after 13.1 overs.

Shoaib Malik was next in, but Pakistan managed only another eight runs before Botha struck again. This time, opening batsman Nazir, who had crawled to 24 off fifty-one balls, copied his captain by edging Botha to Morgan at slip. Malik was next out, in the twenty-first over. After scoring only nine runs from his twenty-five deliveries, he was caught behind by keeper Niall O'Brien, off a slower delivery from his brother Kevin. Pakistan were now 72 for 6, with wicketkeeper Kamran Akmal the only recognised batsman left to bat. Akmal was joined in the centre by Azhar Mahmood.

Johnston must have been having flashbacks to Trinidad, where the Irish had had South Africa in a similar position in the World Cup warm-up game. In that game, Johnston decided to use all his bowlers, to give everyone a run, but, sensing a giant-killing this time, the skipper decided to bring his main attack back into the action in an attempt to clean up the Pakistan tail. Boyd Rankin duly obliged, taking two wickets in the space of four balls in the thirty-first over. First up was Mahmood, who top-edged a short delivery, to give his captain an easy catch at short-midwicket. Mahmood was soon followed to the pavilion by Akmal, who also fell to a top-edge off a short delivery. This time it was a much more difficult take for Johnston, at full stretch at mid-on, in a catch that was almost a carbon copy of the one that Johnston had almost made against Zimbabwe. In holding on to this chance, he appeared to damage his left shoulder as he came down hard on the turf. Pakistan were on their last legs on 105 for 8 after 30.5 overs.

Responsibility now lay on the shoulders of pace bowlers Mohammad Sami and Rao Iftikar to steer the Pakistanis to a respectable total, and they battled gamely, forming a partnership of twenty-five as they pushed on to 130. But Kyle

Andrew White celebrating taking the wicket of Inzamam ul-Haq

Niall O'Brien leaves the field in dejection despite putting in a man of the match performance against Pakistan

McCallan put an end to that partnership in the forty-fourth over as Sami hit a sweep to deep-backward-square straight into the hands of Jeremy Bray, who made no mistake. Umar Gul was last man in, and McCallan finished him off in his next over, the forty-sixth of the innings. Gul tried to hit the ball out of the ground but only managed to find John Mooney at the midwicket boundary. The Irish substitute took an easy catch and followed it up with some fancy footwork, soloing the ball GAA-style before joining his team-mates to celebrate the fall of the final wicket. Pakistan were all out for 132.

It was a phenomenal effort by the Irish, with the only negative being the number of extras – twenty-nine – that were given away. Would these twenty-nine runs be the difference between historic victory and valiant defeat? A break for lunch was time enough to let what had just happened sink in. The Irish bowling figures were outstanding, with André Botha putting in one of the best spells in one-day-international history, with his figures of 8–4–5–2, an unbelievable average of 0.62 runs per over. Only four bowlers had bettered that in one-day internationals where the bowler had bowled eight overs or more. In fact, the list is topped by the next Ireland coach, Phil Simmons, who bowled ten overs for three runs, also against Pakistan, taking four wickets in the process. The new coach will have been taking note of Botha's performances for the future. Rankin also impressed, finishing with figures of 9-1-32-3. Johnston, McCallan and Langford-Smith were also very economical, all averaging 3.1 or less.

Jeremy Bray and William Porterfield walked out after the break knowing that a half-decent partnership was all that was needed virtually to guarantee Ireland victory. Bray would have been full of confidence after his century in the opening game, and Porterfield would have been looking to make amends for his early dismissal against Zimbabwe. However, this time out was a different proposition from the Zimbabwe game. Pakistan were without two of their best bowlers, Akhtar and Asif – their first-choice new-ball pair – who had been left out of the squad due to injury. The pair had also tested positive for the anabolic steroid nandrolone in 2006, and it was rumoured that Pakistani officials feared that they would be targeted by the ICC at the World Cup, as there may have been traces of the banned substance still in their systems. Despite the absence of two quality players, Pakistan's attack was still world class, and even a modest total of 132 was a daunting task for the Irish.

Umar Gul opened the bowling for Pakistan, sharing the new ball with Mohammad Sami. With both bowlers capable of regularly bowling above 85 mph, the Irish batsmen would have their work cut out for them. By the end of the third over, the Irish duo had managed only seven runs between them. The required run rate was only 2.66 runs per over, so there was no need to panic, it was all about keeping wickets in hand. But Bray went for 3 to the first ball of the fourth over, being trapped lbw by Sami, although the ball appeared to be going over the top of the stumps – umpire Brian Jerling not having the benefit of Hawk-Eye. Eoin Morgan came in at number three, again a bit earlier than he would have liked, and lasted only five balls. Like Bray, he too was bowled leg-before by Sami, this time Jerling getting it spot on. The Middlesex man was out for two. With less than six overs gone, and with 118 runs still required, Ireland had already lost two wickets. The confidence that had been there at lunchtime had suddenly evaporated, and Adrian Birrell's side knew that their work was far from complete.

The Party Stand was full; on closer inspection, it was clear that most of the punters in there were full as well. There was a great mix of Irish accents, north and south, cheering on the boys in green, with everyone making an effort to wear their colours. The funny thing was that, although everyone was cheering on the team, no one knew what to sing: was it an 'Olé, olé, olé, olé', a 'Come on you boys in green' or an 'Ireland's Call' moment? The DJ's musical interludes kept everyone happy. (While the Party Stand was great craic, it wasn't the best place to watch cricket, as you were square to the wicket and couldn't really tell what the bowling was doing.)

Niall O'Brien swaggered into the centre with the look of a man in form, although recent forays with the bat suggested otherwise. The Northants keeper wasted no time getting his eye in and started to score immediately, taking Ireland past the fifty-run mark, with Porterfield helping to build the partnership despite his slow scoring. Inevitably, Porterfield

Ireland's Trent Johnston ceremoniously hands the ball to umpire Billy Bowden after he caught out Pakistan's Azhar Mahmood

was next to go but was unlucky with the dismissal: he played on to his stumps off the spin bowling of Hafeez. Porterfield managed only 13 off fifty deliveries but played a huge part in establishing the partnership with O'Brien and moving the score on to 62 before he was dismissed.

Ireland were still in control as Botha came in at number five. With the score on 62 for 3, it was still Ireland's game for the taking. However, three overs later, having faced just six balls, Botha was dismissed, again by Jerling, in one of the worst umpiring decisions in recent memory. Sami's delivery was careering down Botha's leg side, where it caught the all-rounder's pad and rebounded to Hafeez at short-leg, who juggled the ball twice before catching it as he fell, happy with the fact that he had saved the single. Sami, showing Pakistan's ever-increasing anxiety, decided to throw in a big appeal. Jerling must have thought that there was some bat on the ball, as he sent Botha packing. Botha looked bemused, while O'Brien, watching from the non-striker's end, looked even fierier than ever, if that is possible. It was a shocking decision by Jerling, and could prove very costly: Ireland were now in a bit of trouble on 70 for 4.

O'Brien was joined by his brother Kevin and quickly resumed where he had left off, bringing up his fifty off seventy-four balls, thanks to some classic strokes to all parts of the ground. Kevin was taking his time allowing Niall to build up the score. Wickets in hand were vital now that the Duckworth Lewis system was in play and the light was fading rapidly. Ireland were well ahead on this system, which uses a mathematical formula to decide what score a team would need to be at to win a game that is cut short by the weather. The O'Brien boys were playing through the ever-decreasing light, throwing the odd glance skywards and at the umpires. The umpires eventually took the hint and offered the batsmen the light. The O'Briens said thank you very much and jogged off to the pavilion to a standing ovation from the Irish supporters and the team, who were spilling out of the balcony. At this stage, Ireland would win the game if no more play took place; the reserve day would not be used, as the twenty-over mark in the second innings had been passed.

The light improved – barely – and the O'Briens returned to finish the job. The revised target was now 128 off forty-seven overs. This seemed a bit unfair on the Irish, who only got the equivalent of five runs from the three lost overs. Kevin eventually got off the mark after seventeen balls, while Niall continued to tear through whatever bowling attack was thrown at him. He had moved on to sixty-six when the off-break spinner, Shoaib Malik, was brought into the attack to slow things down. His first four balls kept Niall quiet, but the fifth was sent flying back over his head for the first six of the game. O'Brien danced down the wicket to smash the ball into the Headley Stand and move Ireland to within twenty of the target. Malik's last ball of the over was treated with the same distain by O'Brien, who, with victory in his mind, charged down the wicket. Malik spotted him coming and got the ball past him, where Akmal was waiting for an easy stumping. A sudden rush of blood to the head had sent Niall O'Brien back to the pavilion; the innings he had just played deserved a more noble finish than for the batsman to be face-down on the pitch as the bails were taken off his wicket. O'Brien would surely have loved to have been there at the end, but with only twenty required and plenty of wickets to spare, surely the remaining batsmen would finish the job.

Six balls later, two more wickets had been lost. Ireland were now 113 for 7, after Andrew White went for 4, gloving Rao Iftikhar's short delivery to Hafeez at the wicket. Iftikhar's next delivery got rid of Kyle McCallan, who edged to Younis Khan at first slip. Ireland still needed fifteen from seventy-two balls, with three wickets in hand. It was now up to Kevin O'Brien, who had been in for more than ten overs, to see his team home with the new man in, captain Trent Johnston, to give him a dig out.

Iftikhar was on a hat-trick, and Inzamam brought the field in to help his bowler. It wasn't to be: he delivered a wide ball, to knock another run off the Ireland target. Johnston either wanted to finish the game off in record time or was feeling a bit edgy: he swung and missed two of his opening deliveries. O'Brien grabbed a quick single, to reach 16 and tie the game, with Johnston now on 3 off thirteen balls. O'Brien punched the air in delight and waved at the crowd as he avoided the run-

John Mooney does a celebratory Gaelic football style solo after he caught out Umar Gul of Pakistan

out, knowing that the victory was almost assured. But it was, fittingly, the skipper who was to hit the winning runs. With only one needed off the thirty-three balls remaining, Johnston picked up the slower delivery by Mahmood and smashed the ball over mid-wicket and into the stand for the second six of the day, to give Ireland the victory – and at the same time cause the biggest upset in World Cup history. Ireland finished on 133 for 7, to win by three wickets and knock Pakistan out of the World Cup.

Sabina Park erupted. Trent Johnston kept running after hitting his six, while the rest of the Irish squad came bounding down the pavilion steps to congratulate the men in the middle. The TV screen showed Bob Woolmer packing his bag in the Pakistan pavilion. After losing their opening two games, it was all over for the number-four-ranked team. Ireland now had one foot in the Super Eights and were thoroughly enjoying their lap of honour as they celebrated with the Blarney Army, which, perhaps remarkably, given the amount of drink its members had consumed, was still in fine fettle eight hours after the start of proceedings.

The Blarney Army had done Ireland proud and had established itself as part of Ireland's success at the World Cup. The players' reaction showed that it had played a huge part in getting the team home against Pakistan and in keeping their spirits alive against Zimbabwe.

ANDREW WHITE:

The whole crowd experience was amazing. I think the Zimbabwe experience lifted the crowd for the Pakistan game, which was crucial for St Patrick's Day. There is no doubt about it in my mind: the crowd drove us on to the tie in the first game and the victory against Pakistan. The fans who were there realised that they were in the land of partying and fun. They took the West Indian people along with them and really captured their imagination, as we did on the field. There's no doubt that they had a special impact on the tournament.

Man of the match Niall O'Brien received his award on the pitch as TV pictures showed the unprecedented footage of an Irish cricket team being lauded on the world stage. The press conference was packed for the Irish coach, its captain, and its new-found hero, Niall O'Brien, who had found his form with the bat at the perfect time. Bob Woolmer and Inzamam didn't hang around for too long, and left the Irish contingent to enjoy their moment in the world spotlight.

NIALL O'BRIEN:

It was just a game of cricket for me. They had the ball and I had the bat. When you're in the middle, you don't think too much. But to beat a team like Pakistan is a fantastic achievement.

TRENT JOHNSTON:

I didn't do too well in English at school, so I can't think of a word to describe it really. It was just amazing. We bowled in some good areas – and some bad areas as well. Then Niall and Kevin batted fantastically well. And the support we got was magnificent. They had the quality bowlers, and we're not used to this kind of pressure. The way the O'Brien brothers batted, I can't praise them enough. We just had to get back to basics and play as straight as we could. I know I came out swinging like a lunatic, but we knew we had enough overs in the bank.

ADRIAN BIRRELL:

Everything was going for us. It was St Patrick's Day. The stands were full of Irish people, and they were so supportive and vocal. We were also lucky that they had players missing, a couple [Asif and Akhtar] with drugs problems and [Shahid] Afridi, who was suspended for our match. We had more luck with the toss, and certainly with the pitch. For some strange reason, we had a green pitch on St Patrick's Day. That was, I suppose, destiny. We were really disappointed in Nairobi not to qualify for the Twenty20 World Cup when we believed that we were the best Associate team. But it spurred us on and, as I said at the time, 'cricket is not this cruel, there's something down the line for us', so we brought the same attitude into the World Cup. The theme of the World Cup was 'there is no glory without hard work', so we just continued working hard, and we all said... let's work hard, let's practise as hard as we can, and maybe something will come [of it].

The Mooney brothers watch from the sidelines of Sabina Park

And so began the mass exodus – *'movement of the people'*, as hometown hero Bob Marley might have put it – from Kingston to Ocho Rios for the mother of all St Patrick's Day parties. All roads led to Ochi as the Ireland team fled from Kingston after hijacking the World Cup. It was late by the time everyone got back to the resort, but the party was only starting at the Jamaica Grande Hotel. The team were fêted like returning heroes as they made their way from the coach into the hotel lobby. It took them the best part of an hour to get from the team bus to where they gathered on stage to lead the chorus in the first of the night's many sing-songs. The Party Stand had been transported en masse to the other side of the island, and the Ireland team mingled freely with family, friends and fans. The bar closed, temporarily, at 2 am but was reopened when the staff realised that no one was leaving. The manager knocked off the music just in time for the latest sing-song. All the auld boys seemed to drift to the edge of the bar, and by the time the first verse of *'Raglan Road'* was over, the whole bar was paying attention. Emmet Riordan from the *Irish Independent* led the charge, as all the old classics were belted out – some graciously, some not so. They kept coming until the bar manager finally called it quits at some stage before the breakfast guests were due to arrive. The new day was dawning as the last of the partygoers and remaining team members rambled across the hotel lobby and to bed.

Ireland v. Pakistan   Umpires: B F Bowden, B G Jerling

Pakistan innings			runs	balls	4s	6s
Imran Nazir	c E J G Morgan	b A C Botha	24	51	3	0
Mohammad Hafeez	c N J O'Brien	b D Langford-Smith	4	6	1	0
Younis Khan	c A C Botha	b W B Rankin	0	3	0	0
Mohammad Yousuf	c W T S Porterfield	b D T Johnston	15	31	2	0
Inzamam-ul-Haq	c E J G Morgan	b A C Botha	1	3	0	0
Shoaib Malik	c N J O'Brien	b K J O'Brien	9	25	2	0
Kamran Akmal	c D T Johnston	b W B Rankin	27	47	4	0
Azhar Mahmood	c D T Johnston	b W B Rankin	2	21	0	0
Mohammad Sami	c J P Bray	b W K McCallan	12	34	1	0
Iftikhar Anjum	not out		8	43	0	0
Umar Gul	c sub	b W K McCallan	1	13	0	0
Extras		3nb 23w 3lb	29			
Total		all out	132			(45.4 ovs)

Bowler	O	M	R	W	Fall of wicket		
D Langford-Smith	10.0	1	31	1	7	Mohammad Hafeez	103	Azhar Mahmood
W B Rankin	9.0	1	32	3	15	Younis Khan	105	Kamran Akmal
A C Botha	8.0	4	5	2	56	Mohammad Yousuf	130	Mohammad Sami
D T Johnston	7.0	1	20	1	58	Inzamam-ul-Haq	132	Umar Gul
K J O'Brien	6.0	0	29	1	66	Imran Nazir		
W K McCallan	5.4	1	12	2	72	Shoaib Malik		

Ireland innings			runs	balls	4s	6s
J P Bray	lbw	b Mohammad Sami	3	13	0	0
W T S Porterfield		b Mohammad Hafeez	13	50	1	0
E J G Morgan	lbw	b Mohammad Sami	2	5	0	0
N J O'Brien	st Kamran Akmal	b Shoaib Malik	72	106	6	1
A C Botha	c Mohammad Hafeez	b Mohammad Sami	0	6	0	0
K J O'Brien	not out		16	53	2	0
A R White	c Mohammad Hafeez	b Iftikhar Anjum	4	3	1	0
W K McCallan	c Younis Khan	b Iftikhar Anjum	0	1	0	0
D T Johnston	not out		9	14	0	1
Extras		1nb 11w 2lb	14			
Total		for 7	133			(41.4 ovs)

Bowler	O	M	R	W	Fall of wicket	
Umar Gul	9.0	0	24	0	7	J P Bray
Mohammad Sami	10.0	0	29	3	15	E J G Morgan
Iftikhar Anjum	10.0	0	29	2	62	W T S Porterfield
Azhar Mahmood	7.4	1	25	0	70	A C Botha
Mohammad Hafeez	4.0	0	15	1	108	N J O'Brien
Shoaib Malik	1.0	0	9	1	113	A R White
					113	W K McCallan

5   Bob Woolmer

Australia were in action against the Netherlands the morning after Ireland knocked Pakistan out of the World Cup. An unscheduled intermission in the television coverage resulted in some breaking news being broadcast from the studio. The anchor led with 'the latest from the Bob Woolmer incident'. We assumed that Woolmer had been sacked or had resigned, and it was a huge shock to hear that the former England international had been rushed to hospital, and that there were unconfirmed rumours that he was dead.

The rumours were later confirmed, and the extraordinary events on the pitch only twenty-four hours before were replaced by the tragic news of the death of a great cricketing man. Woolmer had appeared in relatively good spirits at the post-match press conference and, while he was obviously disappointed, he looked fine and was very relaxed, saying that there were more important things in life than cricket. Woolmer had also hinted that he was considering stepping down from international coaching due to the amount of travel that is required and the hassle involved in living out of hotel rooms. He told the press that he would sleep on his decision and draw no conclusions until then.

Stories quickly began to emerge of Woolmer's chronic health problems, as well as the fact that he was a diabetic. The stress of being coach of the Pakistan team, coupled with the pressure that was already being heaped on the coach in the wake of the defeat by Ireland were generally considered to have taken their toll, and the consensus was that he had died from natural causes. Woolmer had spoken briefly after the final press conference to the BBC's Alison Mitchell, and while he was obviously very disappointed by Pakistan's elimination from the competition, he was more concerned for the people of Pakistan, who had had high hopes of their team doing well at the tournament.

Bob Woolmer:
We batted abysmally, really just made mistake after mistake after mistake. It just compounded, and eventually we were forty to fifty runs short. That's sad because two and a half or three years' work has gone into this, and to fall out like this is very disappointing. I've accepted many bad days in cricket, but I'm just very disappointed for the Pakistan fans, who were desperate for us to do well. I don't really know what to say apart from apologise for the team's performance, because quite frankly, we should have got through, and I thought we had a genuine chance at a higher level if we got through this round. But pressure has told, and we're not going through. My contract runs out on 30 June anyway, so I'll sleep on my future. I have said that I'm reluctant to continue in international cricket, purely from a travelling [point of view] and so on, but I will stick to coaching at a different level. I think a decision's probably been made for me. I don't think that just because I've lost this game, I'm any different as a cricket coach. There are a number of extenuating circumstances in the last six months that have made coaching Pakistan slightly different to [coaching] normal sides. A lot of those things would have to change if I were to continue with Pakistan. But in reality it's just a sad day for Pakistan cricket. I'm part of that, I don't feel very good about it, and we've just got to pick ourselves up tomorrow and get on with it. I try not to make too many decisions on disappointing days, because they tend to be negative decisions, and disappointment means you get negative. When you make negative decisions about your future, I don't think it's very good.

These 'extenuating circumstances' had been very much in evidence at a pre-match reception in the Pegasus Hotel the evening before the game. The event was attended by several members of the Pakistan squad, team officials, and the Pakistan media. Bob Woolmer also attended but, strikingly, sat apart from the Pakistanis and mingled with some Irish journalists on the other side of the room. Woolmer was asked questions by a couple of Pakistani journalists, and he later told the people with him that the reporters in question were out to ruin him and were working on behalf of his biggest critics back in Pakistan,

The Irish squad observe a minute's silence in honour of Bob Woolmer and former President and Chairman of the ICU Bob Kerr, who died in Jamaica

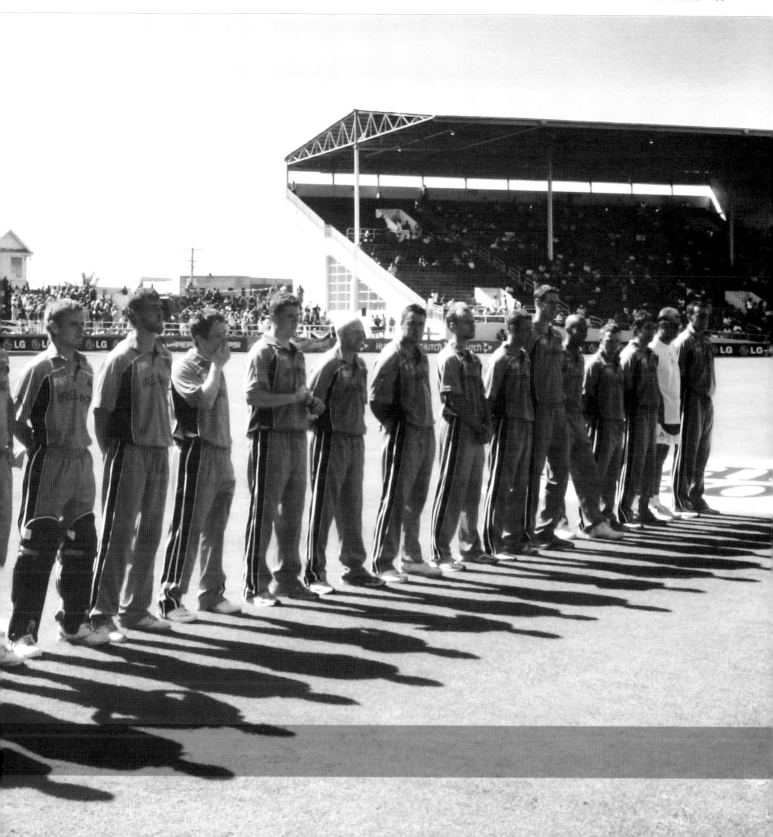

former players Imran Khan and Javed Miandad, and that they would write what they liked no matter what he said to them.

Born in India in 1948, Woolmer played international cricket for England as an all-rounder. His international career yielded only nineteen Tests, which included the Ashes series victory in England in 1977, but he played county cricket for Kent from 1968 to 1984. His international career came to an end when he went on Graham Gooch's rebel tour to South Africa in 1982. It was in South Africa that he made his name as a top-class coach, including a spell with the Cape Town township side Avendale, before he took over at Warwickshire in 1991. He won four trophies at the Edgbaston club; this set him up to take over the South Africa side, who had returned to international cricket after the ending of apartheid. He proved a major success, with the Proteas winning ten out of fifteen Test series and reaching the semi-finals of the 1999 World Cup, where they famously tied with Australia. That final-ball mix-up cost South Africa a place in the final – and Woolmer his job. He then got involved with the ICC to help Associate nations develop, and coached emerging Associate players as part of his role as ICC High Performance Manager. Then, in June 2004, Woolmer returned to the international scene, taking on one of the toughest jobs in sport – coach of the Pakistan national cricket team. He tasted success against in England in the 2005 Test series and was in charge of the side when they famously forfeited a Test match for alleged ball-tampering – the only Test game in history to end in such circumstances. Woolmer was a very good player but will be remembered for what he brought to coaching: he was one of the first people to introduce the use of laptop computers and other technologies to the professional game. At the time of his death, Woolmer had just finished writing a book on coaching, and it was widely rumoured that he would take over the England side after the 2007 World Cup.

Woolmer's death dampened the spirits around the Jamaica Grande Hotel in Ocho Rios, as the Ireland team, who should still have been celebrating their historic victory over Pakistan, looked numbed and subdued as they hung around with family and friends before heading back to Kingston to get back to the cricket. Adrian Birrell was visibly shaken as he obliged the Irish media with some thoughts on the death of his counterpart. Birrell knew Woolmer well: he had studied under Woolmer at a coaching course in South Africa and had got to know him very well during his time at Eastern Province, which had coincided with Woolmer's reign over the national team. Like Woolmer, Birrell put his heart and soul into coaching, and used whatever modern methods were available to help his sides. Birrell believed that the Associate nations in particular owed Woolmer a debt of gratitude for promoting cricket throughout the world.

ADRIAN BIRRELL:

I spoke to him after the game and he was totally gracious in defeat – he made no excuses and praised Ireland's performance. Our paths crossed quite often. I got to know him over the years, and the world will miss a great cricket coach. He had a great playing career but I think he will be remembered for his contribution to coaching. It's ironic that he started the high-performance programme to improve the minor nations, and we were on the outside looking in at that stage. But he has always been a big believer that cricket should be more global. Certainly the 'minnows' will miss him, because he had a lot to do with the progression of more Associate teams in the World Cup. He was very gracious in defeat and he didn't look for any excuses. He just said they didn't play very well and we played very well. I suggested the toss made a big difference, but he didn't think the pitch died down when they bowled, and said if they had batted second they would have still lost. He took it on the chin. Physically, he did look down, but he had just lost a mammoth game and was under immense pressure. It must have had an impact.

Back in Kingston, the tragic news was announced to the media via the excitable Pakistan media manager Pervez Jamil (P.J.) Mir in the lobby of the Pegasus Hotel. Mir graphically described the condition that Woolmer was found in, mentioning that vomit and faeces had also been found at the scene. This was not exactly the type of thing the head of PR should be saying, knowing the type of frenzy that the tabloid press could whip up with such detail. Even Mir was not to know what would transpire over the coming days and weeks, however: this proved to be just the first in a long line of bizarre stories that surfaced as a result of the death of the Pakistan coach.

Later that evening, Mir rounded up the hacks and photographers for a press conference that he was billing as a 'massive story'. The story in question was the surprise resignation of captain Inzamam-ul-Haq from the one-day game and as captain of the Test side. It was no surprise that Inzamam was bowing out of the short form of the game, but the timing of his announcement could only be described as being poor. *The Irish Times'* Richard Gillis was one of the few Irish journalists to attend the conference, as most were back in Ocho Rios celebrating with the team.

RICHARD GILLIS:

How could this be news a few short hours after Woolmer had died? Surely this could have waited. When someone dies, sport becomes an irrelevance. But here we were, with journalists asking questions about greatest memories, high points, great innings. One question summed it up. 'This may sound insensitive, but with Bob Woolmer gone, would it have been better to stay in the job for the sake of stability?' All routine stuff, had it not been for the fact that their coach, a person who had lived and breathed Pakistan cricket for the last three years, had died in tragic circumstances just hours before. Already the story was of succession. Soon after, the circus that is the Pakistan cricket team upped and left the room. The story was out there, Inzamam-ul-Haq had resigned. Big deal. Bob Woolmer was a good man, he deserved better.

A post-mortem was scheduled to take place the following day. With talk of Woolmer suffering from diabetes, coupled with the stress of the result, it was considered, at that stage, that this would be a mere formality. The man in charge of the situation was Scotland Yard's Mark Shields, Jamaica's deputy commissioner of police, who was on a three-year contract with the Jamaican government with a brief to tackle the country's gang violence. Shields was a high-profile figure, having been head of the City of London Police Special Branch, involved with Scotland Yard's Anti-Terrorist Branch, and a member of the National Criminal Intelligence Service's drug and organised-crime unit. His CV was impressive, but the way he handled the investigation into Woolmer's death – an investigation that was soon to become very complex – left a lot to be desired.

The results of the post-mortem proved inconclusive, and further tests were carried out. Then the police announced that they were treating the death as suspicious, and suddenly the world's news press started jetting in to Kingston, and the Pegasus Hotel in particular, to take over from the sports journalists who up to now had been simply reporting on the sad passing of a cricket legend. Rumour after rumour began to do the rounds, as scandal-hungry hacks loitered around the lobby of the hotel asking anyone they could get to stop what was going on and who was involved. A Jamaican journalist got a tip-off and went public, saying that Woolmer had been strangled and that the case was now a murder investigation. There appeared to be a lot of weight behind this building story: the Pakistan team and officials were fingerprinted the following day at the hotel before jetting off to Montego Bay, where they would remain until they were scheduled to leave Jamaica a few days later.

The Jamaican police confirmed the rumours at a press conference, where they announced that Bob Woolmer had been killed by manual strangulation and that they were now looking for the person or persons who had committed the crime. It was also revealed that a bone in Woolmer's neck had been broken in the struggle.

LUCIUS THOMAS

(Police Commissioner of Jamaica): Bob Woolmer died of asphyxiation as a result of manual strangulation. In these circumstances, the matter of Mr Woolmer's death is now being treated as murder.

MARK SHIELDS:

Bob was a large man. It would have taken some significant force to subdue him. I have to say, at this stage, that it looks as if it may be somebody who's somehow linked to him, because clearly he let somebody into his hotel room and it may be that he knew who that person was.

Bob Woolmer and Inzamam-ul-Haq looking dejected after the Ireland defeat

The main theory at this stage was that the murder had to do with match-fixing, with irate bookies planning a hit on the coach. Another story doing the rounds was that there were a couple of fans who had been hanging around the team but now were nowhere to be seen, and that they had got into the coach's room and killed him. The most bizarre rumour was that it was one of the players. Inzamam's name was being bandied about willy-nilly, as if it was only a matter of time before the captain would be charged with the murder of his coach. A row on the team coach on the way back to the hotel after the game was the alleged catalyst for the murder. CCTV was consulted, but proved inconclusive.

Woolmer was honoured with a beautiful tribute before Pakistan's final game against Zimbabwe and again before the Ireland-versus-West Indies encounter. And so the tournament continued. The teams left Jamaica, and with no games scheduled on the island for the best part of a month, the Jamaican police could be left to get on with their investigation. The Pakistan team were cleared of any involvement as they left Jamaica at the end of the group stages, and the police seemed to be no closer to finding a suspect or even a motive for the murder.

The investigation was bolstered by the arrival of a team of officers from the UK, but this was to no avail, and the police were no closer to solving the mystery. It was almost a month before the next twist in the story appeared, this time in the form of BBC's Panorama programme, which suggested that a lethal potion of poison, possibly snake poison, had been used against Woolmer. The venom would have rendered the burly cricket coach helpless, allowing his assailant to strangle him without much of a struggle. And sure enough, who was to turn up in the middle of the programme? Mark Shields, who showed the reporter around a similar room in the Pegasus Hotel, almost recreating the death scene for the benefit of the cameras. This was a bizarre bit of television that seemed fitting for an investigation that had been very badly handled since the morning of Woolmer's death. The only good thing to come out of the latest findings was that Woolmer's body had been flown home for his loved ones to finally get their chance to say goodbye, more than a month after his death. Bob Woolmer was cremated at a private ceremony in his adopted homeland, South Africa.

The story seemed to go away for a few weeks, with no developments in the case until newspaper reports started to quote sources close to the investigation saying that Jamaican police had been told by the UK Home Office pathologist who had flown to Jamaica to probe the death that Woolmer had not been murdered. Jamaican police were very quiet regarding the rumours but eventually admitted that they were studying new material regarding the Woolmer death. Eventually, on 12 June 2007, almost three months since Ireland had beaten Pakistan at Sabina Park, the Jamaican police announced that Bob Woolmer had not been murdered but had died of natural causes. They added that toxicology tests had ruled out the use of any poison. As it turned out, three independent pathologists' reports had concluded that the original finding, of asphyxiation by manual strangulation, had been incorrect. It was also revealed that the bone in the neck that was initially thought to be broken had been X-rayed and was found not to be fractured.

LUCIUS THOMAS:
The JCF [Jamaica Constabulary Force] accepts these findings and has now closed its investigation into the death of Mr Bob Woolmer.

6   Ireland v. West Indies

The last time the Irish travelled in numbers to the Caribbean was back in the bad old days of Cromwell, with his catchy 'to hell or to Connacht' slogan – hell referring to the backwater that was the islands of the Caribbean. A few hundred years later, the 'hell' in question is considered to be one of the most beautiful places on the planet. This time round, nobody was complaining about crossing the Atlantic Ocean.

Irish celebrations were cut short when Jamaica woke up to the terrible news that Bob Woolmer had died. The Irish team were all in Ocho Rios spending the day with family and friends. While they should have been reliving the previous day's excitement and trawling through newspaper reports of their heroics, they were instead left to contemplate the death of the man who had coached the side they had just beaten. The team returned to Kingston that evening and found themselves in the middle of the media scrum that had turned up to the Pegasus Hotel to cover the story.

The rain arrived shortly after the team, and it hung around all week. With almost a week between the Pakistan game and the clash with the West Indies, the players were going mad in their rooms. The swimming pool and tennis courts were no-go areas thanks to the deluge; they couldn't even stroll around the hotel or its grounds without being accosted by one of the assembled hacks trying to get the low-down on the Woolmer affair. Security was heightened, with a patrol on all lifts and every floor of the hotel. It wasn't just the Irish who were affected: the Pakistan, Zimbabwe and West Indies team were also staying in the Pegasus. The Irish team got more bad news during the week as word came through that former ICU president Bob Kerr had died in Ocho Rios.

The team did get to spend a night out in the Blue Mountains at the exclusive Strawberry Hills restaurant owned by Island Records chief Chris Blackwell, a close friend of Bono. The restaurant is perched at the top of the mountains overlooking the sprawling city of Kingston. Unfortunately, the rain put paid to the visual feast below, so the fare being served

up in the kitchen had to suffice. The trip was organised by the Digicel crew, who put on a great night for the squad and the Irish media. Digicel's David Hall presented manager Roy Torrens with a coat of arms of Jamaica and gave each member of the squad a miniature of the Redemption Song sculpture in Emancipation Park. The traditional-Irish musicians and dancers who had been flown over for the St Patrick's Day party performed for the team as their last duty before heading to Norman Manley Airport for the flight back to Ireland. The players were glad to have these distractions, especially after the announcement that Bob Woolmer's death was now being treated as murder.

Getting away from the cricket, Ireland's Andrew White took time out to visit an HIV/AIDS-awareness school for young people with disabilities as part of his role as the Irish team's ambassador for UNICEF. Andrew spent the afternoon at the 3D school, where he chatted with the students and posed for photographs as he helped with the ICC initiative to spread the message of HIV/AIDS awareness: the disease is a major concern throughout the Caribbean.

ANDREW WHITE:

Each one of the competing nations at the World Cup has an ambassador for UNICEF's/ICC's the UNICEF/ICC initiative [to raise] awareness of HIV/AIDS. The ICU chose me as their ambassador for the campaign and it's one that I am very happy to be involved with, as it is a worldwide problem at the minute. A lot of the guys wanted to come along, but there was a training session this afternoon so they couldn't make it. Also our physio, Iain Knox, was very keen to get involved, as he has a medical background... And it's great to do this work in Jamaica as the people here have really got behind the team. They love the way we play with a smile on our face and as a result have been fantastic for us and made us feel really welcome over here.

André Botha cuts one away through the covers against the West Indies

The West Indies had beaten Zimbabwe on the Monday; this meant that victory for Pakistan over Zimbabwe on the Wednesday would send Ireland into the Super Eights. Pakistan played on through the tragedy of losing their coach and, with skipper Inzamam-ul-Haq announcing his retirement from the one-day game, the team were intent on signing off from the tournament with a victory. There was a tribute to Woolmer before the game, and Pakistan won comfortably in the end, with Inzamam taking the catch for the final Zimbabwe wicket, to seal the victory.

KYLE McCALLAN:

We expected to be very competitive against Zimbabwe. That was a game we could win. And our mentality was that if we could win the first game, it would give us two bites of the cherry against the big guns [Pakistan and the West Indies] to qualify out of our group. So the tie against Zimbabwe was a little bit of a let-down... We played poorly, but we showed great courage to come back.

The Ireland players celebrated their qualification to the Super Eights in the captain's hotel room, because of the gaggle of reporters thronging the bars and restaurants of the hotel. It was a low-key affair, with a couple of trays of the nation's favourite brew, Red Stripe, and some takeaway pizza, but the achievement was anything but low key. The players should have been strutting the corridors of the hotel and the streets of Kingston as superstars but instead had to spend their evenings holed up in their rooms watching DVDs and surfing the internet. The game against the West Indies couldn't come quickly enough for them.

The team got a double surprise the day before their final game in Jamaica when they received a letter from the Taoiseach, Bertie Ahern, congratulating them on their achievements. The President of Ireland went one better and called Trent Johnston for a chat about his experiences of the trip. Johnston put the President on speakerphone in the pavilion dressing room in Sabina Park, and the team gathered around to listen to the moving and sincere tribute she paid to the team and what they had done for Ireland on the world stage. She also had heartfelt words of condolence about Bob Woolmer and Bob Kerr, which

were very well received by the players. The team timed a big 'thank you' for the President perfectly, before going off for their final training session in Jamaica.

It was a scorcher on the morning of the game, probably the hottest day since the squad had arrived in Jamaica. What had been billed as Ireland's farewell to the Caribbean turned out to be the start of the second phase – a clash of the top two in the group, with the winners taking two points into the Super Eights. As expected, Trent Johnston would sit this one out due to his shoulder injury, so Kyle McCallan took on the captain's role for the day, and John Mooney came into the team in place of the skipper. McCallan won the toss and bravely chose to bat first, hoping to utilise the good batting conditions before the showers which had been forecast for the afternoon. Once more the Blarney Army turned up in force, but they were placed in the unfamiliar position of being in the minority, as the locals came out to support their team, who had hit some form after beating Pakistan and Zimbabwe. The attendance was just short of 12,000. Sabina Park holds 21,000 when it is full; compared to the attendances at most of the other group games, this was a bumper crowd.

The umpires were Kiwi Billy Bowden and Ian Gould from England, with Brian Jerling as third umpire. Jerling had made some dubious decisions in the Ireland v. Pakistan game, so it was little surprise that he was not out in the middle for this game. The lack of grass on the wicket was no surprise either. The West Indies, being the hosts, were going to dictate conditions as much as was legally possible: they had prepared a grassy wicket for the Ireland v. Pakistan game and a fast, bouncy track for their encounter with Ireland.

Bray and Porterfield opened for the third game in a row, and this time their opening partnership was just three. Porterfield was first to go, edging a Darren Powell delivery to Chris Gayle at first slip. The opening partnership had yet to reach double figures at the World Cup, and Eoin Morgan was getting used to arriving with the new ball very much intact. Jerome Taylor shared the new ball with Powell, and there was clearly a bit of bounce in the wicket as Taylor's short delivery sailed past Bray and over wicketkeeper Denesh Ramdin for four byes.

At last, Eoin Morgan started to look like the batsman that everyone was predicting big things from as he quickly got into his stride, while Bray put the bad decision of the Pakistan match behind him and resumed where he had left off against Zimbabwe, playing some classy shots, including several fluent cuts through the covers. Morgan hit the first six of the game in the fifth over, using Taylor's pace to top-edge the delivery high over the keeper and easily clear the boundary.

Despite the early loss of a wicket, it was a super start by the Irish, who reached 50 after 10.2 overs. The decision to bat first was proving the correct one, and shortly afterwards Bray and Morgan brought up their fifty partnership. But Morgan went with the score on 61. The left-hander skied a top-edge off a Powell delivery. The ball flew high over the wicketkeeper and slips, but there was enough air on it to allow Ramdin to win a three-man, forty-yard chase to glove the ball close to the North Stand boundary. Niall O'Brien was next in. He got going quickly, scoring two boundaries, which took him into double figures. The hero of the Pakistan game couldn't build on the start, however, and was out after edging an Ian Bradshaw delivery to Ramdin.

André Botha joined Bray in the middle but they could only manage six runs between them before Bray, approaching his second World Cup half-century, hit a straight drive off a slower Taylor delivery straight to the sub, Lendl Simmons, at mid-off. Bray had earlier been dropped by Samuels but this time the fielder made no mistake. The opening batsman was sent back to the pavilion nine short of his fifty. Ireland were now 82 for 4 after twenty-two overs. With the run rate standing at almost four an over and with plenty of wickets in hand, it was down to Botha and Kevin O'Brien to push on and attempt to build a decent total. A change of bowlers slowed the run rate right down, though, with Dwayne Bravo and Chris Gayle making it difficult for the Irish to score. Both O'Brien and Botha reached double figures, but by the time O'Brien was out – caught by Ramnaresh Sarwan off Gayle   in the thirty sixth over, the rate had fallen below 3.6. O'Brien had received forty-six deliveries to score his seventeen runs and, likewise, Botha needed fifty-six balls for his 28 before he was out, giving Gayle his second wicket, Ramdin taking the catch off a top-edge.

Ireland were now 139 for 6 with ten overs remaining, and it was up to the tail to try to push on to somewhere near 200. Once Gayle's ten overs (10-0-23-2) were complete, Kyle McCallan and Andrew White started to increase the rate. The momentum was lost, though, due to the heavy rain, which caused a break in play that lasted more than an hour, with Ireland on 161 for 6 after 45.2 overs. The game was reduced to forty-eight overs, which put an end to any hopes the Irish had of getting over 200. The break obviously distracted White, who was out three balls after the restart, attempting a cheeky flick off a Bravo delivery; he missed, and the ball took out the middle stump. John Mooney came out for his World Cup debut with the bat, to face Bravo's last ball of the over. The rising delivery clipped Mooney's glove and flew straight into the hands of Ramdin behind the sticks, leaving Mooney out for a golden duck. Bravo missed out on a hat-trick, and David Langford-Smith hung on with McCallan for the final two overs. Langford-Smith hit eight off seven balls, while McCallan also impressed, hitting 20 from twenty-four deliveries, to give Ireland a respectable total of 183 for 9 off forty-eight overs.

Chris Gayle and Shivnarine Chanderpaul set about chasing the runs with a real sense of purpose. The total had been revised upwards to 190 as Ireland were given the benefit of the doubt for their cautious middle-innings overs. This was probably a fair assessment, considering that Ireland only had Boyd Rankin left in the pavilion at the end of their forty-eight overs.

Gayle looked like he was running late for an appointment, judging by the way he came out swinging his bat. It was a Friday, and there was probably a party somewhere in Kingston, his hometown, with his name on it. Gayle hit three fours in the fourteen balls he faced before holing out to Andrew White off Langford-Smith in the fifth over. Chanderpaul, on the other hand, was in no rush. He steadily built his innings and struck up a great partnership with next man in, Ramnaresh Sarwan. The Guyanese pair easily dealt with the new ball and pushed past fifty in the tenth over, thanks in particular to four boundaries off one Boyd Rankin over. The Irish bowling attack had very little to challenge the duo. Chanderpaul scored freely, with some classic shots, while Sarwan took his time, keeping Chanderpaul on strike.

André Botha and John Mooney came into the bowling attack, but Chanderpaul was seemingly invincible, smashing Botha for six on his way to a fifty-two-ball half-century. The Windies eased past 100, to leave only ninety to win. The century partnership more or less signalled the end of the contest. Chanderpaul hit four sixes in total, with Mooney, McCallan and Botha, again, all on the receiving end of his ferocious batting display. Sarwan got in on the act, smashing McCallan for six before getting out three balls later after McCallan tempted him again; this time Kevin O'Brien was on hand to take the catch at deep-midwicket. The partnership of 119 was eventually broken, but at that stage it was too late: the Windies were on the verge of victory. Marlon Samuels saw things home with Chanderpaul: the former hit 27 off thirty-one deliveries to seal the victory. Chanderpaul was unbeaten on 102. Samuels's quick scoring almost ruined his teammate's chance of a century, but the opening batsman reached the milestone off 108 balls, which included ten fours and four sixes. There was no argument about Chanderpaul being named man of the match.

At the end of the press conference, Chanderpaul even found a bit of time to give the Irish press a heads-up on their next destination, his hometown of Georgetown. There was a roar of laughter when he recommended that they visit Sheriff Street on their trip, as it was a lively place. So the West Indies would take the two points into the Super Eights, leaving Ireland to reflect on some good individual performances but an overall team performance that was unable to handle the brilliance of Chanderpaul. Despite the heavy defeat, there were many positives to be taken out of the game for the Irish. Langford-Smith and McCallan both bowled very economically, averaging 3.67 and 3.5 respectively. All bar one of the top eight batsmen reached double figures, with Jeremy Bray, once again, showing his class, and Botha, McCallan, Morgan and Kevin O'Brien all having decent knocks. What Ireland needed was another performance like Bray's from the Zimbabwe game, or Niall O'Brien's from the Pakistan game, to hold the innings together. With every game from here on in being against quality opposition, coach Adrian Birrell would be challenging his top players to step up to the mark and make themselves counted if they were to have any chance of winning a game or two in the remainder of the tournament.

JEREMY BRAY:

I really believed that the West Indies could have been beaten, it's just a shame that we didn't play that well. We had our moments in that game, when we could have – and should have – posted a decent total, but we didn't bat that well. But as for the game itself, to play in front of a massive crowd and to be in Jamaica itself was awesome. In fact, the three games in Jamaica, to be playing in Sabina Park and the electricity of the place, was probably the best that I have ever experienced. And the massive Irish crowd there was just brilliant. Also the Jamaican people got behind us. They enjoyed the way we played the game. We play with great intensity and smiles on our faces, while a lot of the bigger teams don't, and even in defeat we held our heads up high, and that was the reason why the locals got behind us.

The team put the defeat behind them as they prepared for their final night in Kingston and Jamaica before heading on to Guyana. Digicel threw a big bash at Mas Camp in Kingston – free-in for all the Irish – as a way of sending the players off on their adventure in the Super Eights and sending the Blarney Army home in style after two weeks in Jamaica. It was a who's who in the bar of the Pegasus Hotel that night, with all the West Indies team and the Ireland players having a drink and a chat. And footballers Dwight Yorke, Sol Campbell and Andy Cole were all in town to support their mate Brian Lara. Yorke had actually wandered into the wrong hotel room on the infamous twelfth floor the day before. Instead of finding Lara, he was accosted by *Irish Independent* journalist Emmet Riordan, looking for a scoop. Yorke, who plays for Roy Keane's Sunderland, made a hasty retreat, but Riordan did manage to get a couple of lines out of the former Manchester United legend.

DWIGHT YORKE:

Yeah, I'll be at the game tomorrow. I'll be supporting the West Indies. But don't tell the Gaffer.

William Porterfield leaves the field after being caught out by Chris Gayle against the West Indies

Ireland v. West Indies   Umpires: B F Bowden, I J Gould

Pakistan innings			runs	balls	4s	6s
J P Bray	c sub	b J E Taylor	41	72	7	0
W T S Porterfield	c C H Gayle	b D B Powell	0	2	0	0
E J G Morgan	c D Ramdin	b D B Powell	18	34	0	1
N J O'Brien	c D Ramdin	b I D R Bradshaw	11	19	2	0
A C Botha	c D Ramdin	b C H Gayle	28	56	1	1
K J O'Brien	c R R Sarwan	b C H Gayle	16	46	1	0
A R White		b D J Bravo	18	29	0	0
W K McCallan	not out		20	24	2	0
J F Mooney	c D Ramdin	b D J Bravo	0	1	0	0
D Langford-Smith	not out		8	7	1	0
Extras		2nb 6w 4b 11lb	23			
Total		for 8	183			(48.0 ovs)

Bowler	O	M	R	W	Fall of wicket	
J E Taylor	8.0	0	37	1	3	W T S Porterfield
D B Powell	9.0	2	24	2	61	E J G Morgan
I D R Bradshaw	9.0	0	27	1	76	N J O'Brien
D J Bravo	7.0	1	34	2	82	J P Bray
C H Gayle	10.0	0	23	2	129	K J O'Brien
M N Samuels	5.0	0	23	0	139	A C Botha
					163	A R White
					163	J F Mooney

West Indies innings			runs	balls	4s	6s
C H Gayle	c A R White	b D Langford-Smith	18	14	3	0
S Chanderpaul	not out		102	113	10	4
R R Sarwan	c K J O'Brien	b W K McCallan	36	71	2	1
M N Samuels	not out		27	31	3	1
Extras		6w 1lb	7			
Total		for 2	190			(38.1 ovs)

Bowler	O	M	R	W	Fall of wicket	
D Langford-Smith	9.0	1	33	1	24	C H Gayle
W B Rankin	5.0	0	38	0	143	R R Sarwan
A C Botha	6.0	0	35	0		
J F Mooney	4.0	1	22	0		
W K McCallan	10.0	0	35	1		
K J O'Brien	3.0	0	13	0		
A R White	1.1	0	13	0		

Niall O'Brien narrowly avoids a run out in his 63-run haul against England at Providence Stadium in Guyana

been fantastic. The pavilion was open for business as the team trained, and the local members looked on as the Irish lads got a good going-over in the field. Former West Indies player Lance Gibbs was there as well: the spin-bowling legend had returned to his hometown, where a street was being named in his honour.

The stadium in Georgetown – the Providence Stadium – is situated on the outskirts of the city, about a fifteen-minute drive from the Irish team's hotel. The stadium had been built specially for the World Cup and was partly funded by the Indian government. It has a capacity of 20,000 and has replaced the Bourda as the main cricket venue in the country. Ireland were scheduled to play three games in Guyana, against England, South Africa and New Zealand, but on their arrival it was rumoured that the new stadium was not completed, and that there was a chance that the games would be moved to Trinidad or, bizarrely, back to Jamaica. However, the first game between South Africa and Sri Lanka passed with no problems. It turned out to be one of the most memorable matches of all time, as Sri Lankan fast bowler Lasith Malinga took four wickets from four consecutive deliveries in a thrilling climax to the contest, which South Africa just edged. The Ireland team actually went along to watch the game to get a look at the venue. As the end approached, with South Africa cruising, Jeremy Bray suggested that they leave early to avoid the traffic. Sure enough, the team got back to the hotel to find out that they had just missed history being made back at the stadium: they were on the team bus when Malinga did his business. Several members of the Irish media, who were enjoying a rare day off, also left the game early to see if the Windies Sports Bar in Georgetown was showing the Ireland Euro 2008 qualifier from Croke Park. Sure enough, RTÉ wasn't piped into the pub, and they had to watch the cricket match they had just left. At least they managed to catch Malinga's haul – albeit on television.

The locals in Guyana took to the Irish in much the same way as they had in Jamaica. The cricket-loving Georgetown folk spoke highly of the Irish team, and they were very impressed with the approach that the team took to every game.

With seventeen nights to spend in Georgetown, it is safe to say that many DVDs were watched by the Irish team during their stay. The Cara Lodge was a beautiful hotel, with great food and a lovely relaxed ambience throughout, but there was very little to keep the players occupied. There was no tennis court or swimming pool, and if any of the players wanted to leave the hotel, they had to be accompanied by one of the armed guards who patrolled the hotel around the clock.

The ennui got the better of Eoin Morgan one day, as he asked a policeman for a go of his rifle. The guard obliged, handing the rifle to Morgan, who posed for a photograph before handing the firearm back. The photo was taken by media manager Barry Chambers, and the next day it turned up on the front page of the Irish newspapers, and the policeman was relieved of his duties.

BARRY CHAMBERS:

My photo was printed on the front page of a few of the papers in Ireland. It got picked up on the Internet and, given the global nature of communications nowadays, winged its way back to Guyana – hence my horror at seeing it on the main National Guyana news bulletins with an accompanying story about a policeman being sacked. What had started out as a bit of fun had now turned serious. I spoke with Frank Matthews, our police liaison officer, and he set up a meeting with the head of the Guyana Police Department. Adrian Birrell, Matt Dwyer and myself met with him, and Adi pleaded on behalf of the squad that he be reinstated. He spoke, as Adi does, from the heart, and very eloquently, and the police chief gave his assurance that he wouldn't be sacked and that we would put the incident down to 'World Cup fever'. The squad gave him a couple of signed shirts to apologise for the trouble caused.

The players did manage to get a few outings. Phil Simmons knew a local jeweller who promised the players a good deal on all things gold, so no doubt a few early Christmas presents were purchased for the WAGs. The players also got to sample many of the decent restaurants around town, with Buddy's Chinese restaurant being one of the favourites. And the hotel owner organised a party for the team and media at his beautiful house out on the Georgetown coast.

The team also got to visit the country's main tourist attraction, the Kaieteur Falls – one of the most powerful waterfalls in the world. The drop is more than 700 feet, which makes it five times higher than Niagara Falls and twice the height of Victoria Falls. To get there, you can either hike for five days or take a one-hour flight from Georgetown. The only problem was that the aeroplanes looked a little bit the worse for wear: rickety old ten-seaters that don't necessarily inspire confidence. Irish bowler Boyd Rankin – standing at 6 foot 8 inches – was a bit cramped, to say the least. But once we arrived, we forgot all about the plane journey and marvelled at what truly is a wonderful sight to behold. The guide, Colin Benjamin, gave a fine commentary walking through the rainforest, which led to a ledge overlooking the Falls. The noise of the water crashing below was deafening: the flow was almost at full strength as it raged over the ledge. The water in these parts is full of iron, and from a distance the falls looks like a pint of Guinness being poured. Mr Benjamin was obviously very proud of the area and made sure that we didn't drop any litter or remove anything precious – like stones or the little golden frogs that were hopping around the foliage. 'All you take is photos, and all you leave are footprints' was his motto.

KYLE McCALLAN:

Kaieteur Falls was special. If you ever go to Guyana, you have to see the Kaieteur Falls.

The Digicel office had only recently set up in Georgetown; this was a big boost for the travelling Irish. Normally when you land in a strange country, you find the main Irish bar and talk to the staff to find out the best places to eat and drink. Well, if you're ever in the Caribbean, find the Digicel crowd and you won't be too far away from the party. Mia from Carlow, Michael from Templemore, and Aidan from Kilmacud helped with any phone issues, provided local SIM cards, organised nights out, and recommended all the best places to eat and drink. This was a big help to the remaining Irish media, most of whom arrived in the country without a place to stay or any local currency. The nightlife in Georgetown is spectacular, with lots of beautiful restaurants and great bars, not to mention the Palm Court nightclub, which was frequented more than once by the travelling hacks and the odd player or two.

Paul Mooney sitting by the magnificent Kaieteur Falls in Guyana

8   Ireland v. England

While Jamaica was rocking on St Patrick's night after Ireland's famous victory against Pakistan, over in St Lucia another Irishman was leafing through the World Cup script to see if he had missed a few pages. Ed Joyce was instrumental in Ireland's qualification for the World Cup, averaging 100 in the 2005 ICC Trophy, but now he would have to face his former team-mates in the same tournament – but this time with three lions on his shirt.

Damien Joyce, Ed's brother, was one of the thousands of Irish partying in Jamaica, and another sibling, Dominick, had just missed out on making the Ireland squad after hitting a dip in form in the build-up to the tournament. In fact, five of the Joyce family have represented Ireland at cricket, so for Ed to come up against Ireland at the World Cup so soon after switching allegiance must have been pretty difficult for him to come to terms with. And it showed.

Joyce, in demand by both the English and Irish media – or what was left of the Irish media, as half of them had gone back after the Jamaica leg as editors back in Ireland wouldn't finance another four weeks in the Caribbean for them – was duly paraded in front of the cameras and waiting hacks at the Meridien Pegasus hotel to tell his story two days before the Ireland v. England Super Eight clash in Guyana.

Joyce had been bowled for a duck against New Zealand in the World Cup opener but had come good against the weaker teams in the group, to help guide England into the Super Eights. He hit 66 against Canada and was man of the match against Kenya, putting in an impressive knock of 75 as England won by seven wickets. The English media went easy on him: they seemed to take it as a given that he would jump at the chance to play for them, so they were treating it as a novelty story, as they would if Kevin Pietersen had been playing

against South Africa. The Irish media, for the most part, were on first-name terms with Joyce but still had to ask the questions that the now cricket-mad Irish public was asking back home. How can an Irishman play for England, and how can he play for England in the World Cup against the country of his birth?

Joyce, flanked by the England media manager, was well versed for such questions and answered most of them before they were even asked.

ED JOYCE:
I made my decision four or five years ago to do what I've done, and I'm happy with that. Back then, Ireland weren't playing many games against the big teams and it doesn't look like we are going to get Test status any time soon. It's still going to be strange, obviously, playing against my own countrymen, but I've got to get runs in every game. It's probably more helpful that I know ten or eleven of the Irish guys and they only know me, but I'm hoping that if I do what I do well it won't make any difference.

And while Joyce felt that he had no option but to seek to further his career by declaring for England, he was quick to deflect the attention from himself onto the current crop of Irish-born players who would be eyeing up an England call-up in the future.

ED JOYCE:
People like Eoin Morgan and Niall O'Brien probably have a slightly different decision to make now that they have a few options.

Joyce was, however, visibly delighted that Irish cricket had made such an impact, and was aware that he was one of the main reasons for its recent revival.

Niall O'Brien plays a sweep shot in front of England's wicket keeper Paul Nixon

ED JOYCE:

It's a massive credit to everyone on the team that they got through to the second round. Personally, I think it's great for the tournament that there are a couple of teams in the Super Eights that weren't expected to make it through. I don't agree with the people who are suggesting that it's bad for the game, I can't possibly see why they would say that, because who wants to see the same teams play each other all the time?

Joyce emerged from the press conference unscathed and made his way over to the rest of his 'countrymen' who were waiting for him in the hotel lobby, where they shared a joke before disappearing onto the team bus to training.

Joyce had actually played against Ireland in his first game for England at Stormont in June 2006. He had managed to score only ten runs in front of one of the biggest crowds ever to turn up to a cricket match in Ireland. Around seven thousand people packed the Belfast venue to see Ireland almost pull off a shock result. In the end, they lost by just thirty-eight runs in their first official one-day international.

But this time it was the World Cup, and with a bigger scalp – Pakistan – already in the bag, the Irish were in the mood for another shock. Ireland had a week to prepare for this clash with the auld enemy – although it was really just three days when travel and rain had been factored into the equation.

The team was training at the former Test venue, the Bourda, which was a fantastic setting to prepare for a game as big as the England one. Training then moved to the Providence Stadium the day before the game, to give the team a chance to get used to the surroundings. It was a rain-interrupted session, mainly consisting of the now-obligatory touch-rugby clash between the Oldies and the Youngies, followed by some fielding drills, which were exhausting just to look at.

But the main talking point of the day came, naturally enough, at the press conference. Most of the Irish team's press conferences so far had been with coach and captain. A Springbok and an Aussie talking to the world media can give the impression that the team is 'Ireland' in name only.

Niall O'Brien did turn up for the press conference after the Pakistan match, but his accent could easily be mistaken for an English or even an Aussie one – unless you are familiar with the deceptive tones of the Southside Dubliner.

Vice-captain Kyle McCallan turned up to face the English media; a stronger Ulster accent you could not find. Before McCallan had uttered a word, you could tell by his body language, as he sat at the top table, that he had a message for our friends from across the water. Like the rest of the Ireland team, McCallan had been paying close attention to what was being said about the Irish at the tournament. The pre-tournament doubters of Ireland, Michael Holding and Michael Atherton, had already been silenced in Jamaica, but now there was a whole new breed of pundit lining up to take a pop at Ireland's achievements. For some, it seemed that participation in the World Cup was fine but that the Super Eights was a sacred place, reserved only for the elite Test-playing nations. Leading the charge was esteemed BBC cricket correspondent Jonathan Agnew, commentator on the world-renowned *Test Match Special* radio show.

JONATHAN AGNEW:

The Super Eight will be the duller and more predictable as a result of the presence of Ireland and Bangladesh, rather than India and Pakistan. I can't say that I really believe it is for the good of the sport that one of its finest and most passionate contests – India against Pakistan – has now been replaced by Ireland against Bangladesh. Those teams are simply not good enough to compete against Test-class nations with the consistency required to make the World Cup the spectacle it has to be to showcase the game at its best.

The first issue McCallan addressed at the press conference related to the Irishness of the four players in the squad who had been born outside the island of Ireland.

Boyd Rankin celebrates after sending Ed Joyce's off stump flying out of the ground

KYLE McCALLAN:

These guys are not mercenaries who have flown in for the World Cup. They have contributed to Irish cricket over a prolonged period. Trent is married to an Irish girl, with two Irish kids; Jeremy Bray has lived in Ireland as long as I can remember, as has André Botha. People are welcome to their own opinions, but in a small way it motivates us even more, particularly the guys born and bred in Ireland, to show they can compete at this level. We beat Pakistan fairly and squarely. Niall O'Brien scored 72 and Boyd Rankin got 3-30 – two born-and-bred Irishmen.

Andrew White was fighting for his team on the front line; he had his own blog on the BBC website, and he had plenty to say about his BBC 'colleagues' and their indifference to the Ireland team.

ANDREW WHITE:

We are in the Super Eights having tied with Zimbabwe and beaten Pakistan. England, on the other hand, got through but failed to beat the other Test nation in their group, New Zealand. How can anyone argue against our berth in the top eight? There had been a lot of hype beforehand about the nationality of Trent Johnston, Jeremy Bray, André Botha and Dave Langford-Smith, all born outside Ireland but who have set up home and lived in Ireland for many years. The English press are always quick to mention the quartet but always fail to register the birthplaces of Kevin Pietersen, Andrew Strauss, Jamie Dalrymple and our very own Ed Joyce. When will they ever give it a rest? The BBC's pundit Jonathan Agnew said that Pietersen should be making hundreds against 'these people'. This illustrated to us as players what we are battling against, as this comment showed a lack of respect for 'these people' that have added so much to a World Cup that forced the Jamaican public to sing and dance in Sabina Park until the sun had long gone down on St Patrick's Day.

In fairness to the English media, there were just as many journalists and commentators lauding the Irish, their team spirit, their ability to play with a smile on their faces, and the fact that they had brought something new to a World Cup that was quickly gaining a reputation as being one of the worst since the competition's inception in 1975.

Because this was Guyana, there was a good chance that the match would be affected by rain. But on the morning of the match, the sun was beating down on the newly built Providence Stadium. The conditions were perfect for batting, but it was only the second game that had been played at the stadium, so it would have been hard to assess the pitch and how it would play. Trent Johnston was back in the side having missed the West Indies clash with a recurring shoulder injury, which meant that John Mooney was left out to make way for the skipper. England named the same side that had beaten Kenya in the final group game.

The England team was at its strongest, but in world cricketing terms it was a very average outfit. Kevin Pietersen aside, the team that lined out against Ireland would struggle against any of the big names of cricket, as was shown in the New Zealand game in the group stages. Their other two world-class players, Andrew Flintoff and Michael Vaughan, both carrying injuries, were a long way from their best form, and their form player, Ed Joyce, should really have been playing in green. Paul Collingwood and Ian Bell are decent batsmen, and Monty Panesar is proving to be a very handy spin bowler, but looking at the England team as a whole, surely the Irish, especially with the current wave of confidence running through the squad, had this game down as a potential victory. So could Ireland beat England at their own game? It would be like London or New York beating Kilkenny in the All-Ireland hurling final. It simply couldn't happen. Or could it?

If this game had been played in Barbados or Jamaica, it would have probably been sold out, but this was Guyana, and there were no more than 1,500 people at the game, scattered around the magnificent arena. Atmosphere was severely lacking, especially at this early stage of the day: the game started at 9.30 am. The famous Barmy Army failed to show up, since it was England's only game in Guyana, and the Irish fans had long gone following their two-week sojourn in Jamaica.

There were a handful of English fans, recognisable from their St George's crosses, emblazoned with their football team of choice: Notts County were well represented. And the Irish crowd, fifty or so in number, were sitting at the top of the stand

Irish players congratulate Boyd Rankin as Ed Joyce makes his way back to the pavilion

sheltering from the sun. At least they were all sitting together in an attempt to generate a smidgen of noise. Amongst them were the remaining wives and girlfriends, the owner of the hotel where the Irish team were staying, Shaun McGrath from Donegal, his family and friends, and some impostors dressed in green – whether by choice or under orders.

Over in the Party Stand – a far superior grass terrace than the Sabina Park equivalent, and with a great sit-down view from behind the wicket – another bunch of Ireland supporters was enjoying the sunshine and making the most of the eight beer tokens that came with the match ticket. These consisted of an Irish couple who had won a trip on the radio, journalist Philip Nolan, who was over to write a piece for the *Daily Mail*, and the Digicel employees, who had been given the day off work provided they went along to support Ireland. The Digicel people had searched the streets of Georgetown for some Irish paraphernalia but ended up having to stick home-made shamrocks on to T-shirts and hats for the occasion.

England skipper Michael Vaughan won the toss and, as expected, decided to bat, and it was Vaughan and Joyce who opened. The first over from Langford-Smith proved to be no problem for the English batsmen. Boyd Rankin was next to bowl. Rankin took the ball and made his way to his mark to commence his first over. Joyce knew all about Rankin's pace, the two having played together at Middlesex, but he misread the delivery, shouldering arms (not playing a shot and lifting his bat over his shoulder). The noise of his off stump crashing out of the turf sent Rankin jumping for joy as he passed his former team-mate, who turned on his heels and ambled back to the pavilion, head down. Joyce out for one.

BOYD RANKIN:

It was a very special thing [to bowl Ed Joyce] and I couldn't really believe that I got him first ball. I had targeted him before the game, so to get him first ball was unbelieveable. I don't think he was too happy after the game, as he shook hands but didn't say much, so I'll be looking forward to catching up with him in the near future. He's a good lad; it's just a pity that I had to get him first ball [laughs].

Ian Bell was next in, and England started to score, pushing past twenty in the fifth over, but Rankin was bowling superbly and dispatched the England skipper with the second ball of his third over, Vaughan edging another perfect delivery to Niall O'Brien behind the sticks. After three overs, Rankin's figures were 3–1–5–2.

With two wickets down, England were struggling at 23 for 2. The next man in, Kevin Pietersen, was ranked as the best one-day batsman in the world so, despite their impressive start, Ireland still had a long way to go to cause another upset.

Bell was finding it difficult to score, but Pietersen found his groove immediately, pushing on to 30 thanks to Trent Johnston's first over, the twelfth of the innings, going for fourteen runs; the rate already stood at more than five an over. But André Botha, in for Langford-Smith in the thirteenth over, slowed things down, with Johnston also bowling well despite his shaky start. The rate had dropped to four by the time Kevin O'Brien took the ball in the twenty-second over.

Bell was the main reason for the slow rate, and managed just 31 from seventy-four balls before O'Brien sent him packing with his second delivery. Bell looked shocked to be given out, but umpire Simon Taufel had no doubts that he had made contact, Niall O'Brien taking an easy catch behind.

Paul Collingwood was next in for England, and Kyle McCallan came into the Ireland attack, the off-spinner helping to maintain the slow pace with some fine bowling, which eventually led to Pietersen's dismissal, William Porterfield taking a fine catch with Pietersen just two short of his half-century.

At that stage, Ireland were looking good for another shock, with the England top order gone for 113 midway through the twenty-seventh over. With the rate at four an over, the Irish captain would have been hoping to keep England below 220, which would have been a very gettable target. The skipper was also looking for more wickets, and reintroduced Rankin – although Rankin had to pack it in after seven overs because of cramp. This was a big blow to Ireland, considering the way the Ulsterman was bowling, but at the other end McCallan was causing new arrival Andrew Flintoff plenty of problems, with an extremely accurate spell.

McCallan bowled his final over, the forty-first, with impressive figures of 10–0–38–1, leaving England on a disappointing 175 for 4. However, Collingwood and Flintoff had moved on to 38 and 33 respectively and looked pretty comfortable, especially when the pace bowlers came back into the attack.

The next few overs were expensive, but Johnston was rewarded with Flintoff's wicket when the England all-rounder played on to his stumps while trying to guide the ball to third man. This wicket resulted in the first appearance of the now-famous funky-chicken dance in Guyana. Flintoff departed for 43 off sixty-two balls. England were now 194 for 5 after 43.3 overs.

So with just over six overs to go, Collingwood was the only noted batsman left, and he had wicketkeeper Paul Nixon alongside him, with just the tail to follow. But then Ireland's bowling collapsed. The final six overs went for seventy-one, leaving England on 266 for 7 after the fifty overs. Nixon and Collingwood were both dismissed in the last two overs but by then it didn't matter, Collingwood finishing on 90 off eighty-two balls, with Nixon hitting nineteen off fifteen deliveries.

Ireland came out after lunch and lost Jeremy Bray and Eoin Morgan almost immediately, Bray out for a duck, caught at backward point by Ravi Bopara, and Morgan run out for two after some fine fielding by bowler Sajid Mahmood. Ireland were 11 for 2, with less than four overs of their innings gone.

Niall O'Brien, the hero of the Pakistan match, was next in, hoping to repeat the heroics of Sabina Park on St Patrick's Day. At last, a partnership began to build, as Ireland pushed on to 50 for 2 after twelve overs, with O'Brien scoring a quickfire 31 off thirty-six balls before Porterfield was out for 31, off sixty-nine deliveries, looping a Flintoff delivery to Bell. Porterfield's 31 was his highest total of the World Cup so far.

André Botha was next in, but the run rate slowed as Monty Panesar and Michael Vaughan bowled some impressive spin, and the required rate climbed above seven an over. O'Brien eased past fifty, off sixty-six balls, for his second half-century of the World Cup, but the game had started to slip away from Ireland. Then, in the thirtieth over, Botha tried to attack the Panesar bowling but found the safe hands of Flintoff, and was out for 18. Kevin O'Brien came and went for 12, again from Panesar's arm, out lbw, leaving Ireland on 139 for 5 off thirty-six overs. O'Brien senior followed his brother to the pavilion in the next over, being stumped by Paul Nixon after charging down the pitch to Vaughan.

Andrew White and Trent Johnston came in and gave it one last push, scoring fifty from seven overs. Johnston managed two sixes and hit 27 from twenty-one balls, and White hit an impressive thirty-eight from thirty-five balls. The Party Stand was becoming more and more animated as it looked as though the Irish might chase down the total. (By this stage, there was a much healthier crowd inside the stadium – there must have been a gate left unattended somewhere – and the Party Stand was in full swing, the locals giving any English fielder in the vicinity a hard time.)

But it was too late to save the game, as both wickets fell with Ireland still almost sixty runs short of the target. Flintoff took the last two wickets, Langford-Smith and McCallan, to wrap things up with eleven balls remaining, Ireland all out for 218.

TRENT JOHNSTON:

Our 'death' bowling wasn't up to scratch for this standard. Paul Collingwood batted very well and then the two spinners, Michael and Monty, squeezed us in the middle and applied the pressure. We gave it a fight at the end and it's a tribute to the guys when Michael brings back Andrew Flintoff to clean up the tail. We're not used to playing at this level but it's an experience the guys are very much enjoying and we can only learn from this.

MICHAEL VAUGHAN:

I played against Ireland two years ago for Yorkshire and the way they play their cricket these days compared to then is a credit to them – they produced a good game but we always felt the runs we got were going to be too many.

Shamrock Rovers fans missed the start of the football season to support Ireland in the Caribbean

Another valiant effort from the Irish amateurs, but the defeat hit hard, as they knew that a target of 220 or 230 would have given them a real chance of victory. It was actually quite reassuring to see how disappointed the Irish team were as they arrived back at the hotel. They don't do moral victories: they had beaten one of the top teams in the world and wanted more of the same. Nonetheless, the team's confidence took a bit of a hit after the highs of Jamaica, and with no easy matches on the horizon, the next three weeks might prove to be the biggest test that the Ireland team would encounter on this journey in the competition.

Later that evening, the team cheered up and went down to the Windies Bar to relax and unwind. Spirits were lifted as the night wore on, and there was even time for the now-obligatory sing-song upstairs on the balcony, led by Peter Gillespie and Dave Langford-Smith.

Ireland v. England   Umpires: B R Doctrove, S J A Taufel

England innings			runs	balls	4s	6s
E C Joyce		b W B Rankin	1	5	0	0
M P Vaughan	c N J O'Brien	b W B Rankin	6	13	1	0
I R Bell	c N J O'Brien	b K J O'Brien	31	74	2	0
K P Pietersen	c W T S Porterfield	b W K McCallan	48	47	5	0
P D Collingwood	run out		90	82	8	3
A Flintoff		b D T Johnston	43	62	4	0
P A Nixon	c E J G Morgan	b A C Botha	19	15	1	1
R S Bopara	not out		10	5	1	0
S I Mahmood	not out		0	0	0	0
Extras		3nb 13w 2lb	18			
Total		**for 7**	**266**	**(50.0 ovs)**		

Bowler	O	M	R	W	Fall of wicket		
D Langford-Smith	7.0	0	38	0	6	E C Joyce	
W B Rankin	7.0	1	28	2	23	M P Vaughan	
D T Johnston	10.0	0	70	1	89	I R Bell	
A C Botha	10.0	1	56	1	113	K P Pietersen	
K J O'Brien	4.0	0	26	1	194	A Flintoff	
W K McCallan	10.0	0	38	1	245	P A Nixon	
A R White	2.0	0	8	0	258	P D Collingwood	

Ireland innings			runs	balls	4s	6s
W T S Porterfield	c I R Bell	b A Flintoff	31	69	1	0
J P Bray	c R S Bopara	b J M Anderson	0	1	0	0
E J G Morgan	run out		2	7	0	0
N J O'Brien	st P A Nixon	b M P Vaughan	63	88	4	0
A C Botha	c A Flintoff	b M S Panesar	18	39	1	0
K J O'Brien	lbw	b M S Panesar	12	19	1	0
D T Johnston		b A Flintoff	27	21	1	2
A R White	c P A Nixon	b P D Collingwood	38	35	4	0
W K McCallan		b A Flintoff	5	6	0	0
D Langford-Smith	lbw	b A Flintoff	1	2	0	0
W B Rankin	not out		4	8	0	0
Extras		5nb 9w 3lb	17			
Total		**all out**	**218**			**(48.1 ovs)**

Bowler	O	M	R	W	Fall of wicket		
J M Anderson	7.0	1	35	1	6	J P Bray	197	D T Johnston
S I Mahmood	8.0	2	34	0	11	E J G Morgan	209	A R White
A Flintoff	8.1	1	43	4	72	W T S Porterfield	210	D Langford-Smith
P D Collingwood	6.0	0	38	1	116	A C Botha	218	W K McCallan
M S Panesar	10.0	1	31	2	139	K J O'Brien		
M P Vaughan	9.0	0	34	1	139	N J O'Brien		

After arriving in South Africa the team stop off at one of coach Adrian Birrell's favourite haunts, near Port Elizabeth, for a well-earned juice and a local delicacy

9   Ireland v. South Africa

As March gave way to April, the Ireland team, which had left Ireland for South Africa in early January, found themselves having been almost three months on the road. While the benefits of training like a full-time professional cricket outfit had already reaped huge rewards, three months living in each other's pockets must have been taking its toll on the squad and the coaching staff. So when an April Fool's prank was set up to pass the afternoon following training, it was a brave decision, considering that a big bust-up could have made the remaining three weeks more than a little uncomfortable. The Ireland media manager, Barry Chambers, was gently coerced into setting up the prank on the 'spin twins', Kyle McCallan and Andrew White. The two Ulster boys had stepped on a few toes in the pre-tournament trip to South Africa and were happy to be known as the practical jokers in the pack. Chambers was sent off to inform the two lads that an interview had been set up with Christopher Martin-Jenkins – the much-respected BBC journalist who commentates on *Test Match Special* – over lunch at the Windies Bar.

Whether it was the ennui of the hotel bedroom or the hype of the World Cup experience, neither White nor McCallan questioned Chambers – why wouldn't Martin-Jenkins want to interview them? – or thought to look at the calendar, so they agreed immediately, and asked if their respective partners could go along for the lunch appointment. Off they went, and Chambers rang them when they arrived to say that CMJ was running late and would be along shortly, as he had been caught up at the stadium. A while later, the entire team sent the two lads a text wishing them an enjoyable lunch and a happy April Fool's Day. Messrs McCallan and White were not happy as they returned to the Cara Hotel, with vengeance on their mind. Chambers squealed like a pig when his hotel door was beaten down, and the rest of the team were warned that they should be on their guard for the rest of the trip. CMJ was actually commentating on the West Indies v. Sri Lanka game live on the BBC, so if they had been listening to the radio they would have saved themselves an afternoon of waiting – and the price of lunch for four in the Windies Bar.

A few hours later, the incident was over, with both McCallan and White acknowledging that they had been taken for a ride. While this type of incident can divide a group, by training the next day, the team spirit had lifted again, and was now stronger than ever. McCallan and White 'took one for the team' and sent Ireland into the game with South Africa in high spirits and full of confidence.

JEREMY BRAY:

We've been on the road for so long, and it's amazing that there have been no fights or anything, although we do give each other their own space as well. Everyone loves the banter and all, and yes, it can be tough, but it just shows what a good unit we are. Nothing bad has come out of the four months that we have spent together. It's very much a single man's life. It would be nice to get home and have a couple of weeks off, but it's straight back into it. The body needs a rest. But you get to see some of the world's greatest places. I suppose you do get a bit tired in and out of hotels all the time. But it's been an awesome experience, I haven't regretted any of it.

Ireland's opponents for game three of the Super Eights were ranked as the top one-day-international side in the world coming into the tournament, so on paper at least, the game would be Ireland's toughest test yet. South Africa had come through the group stage with no difficulties, beating Scotland and the Netherlands, but had been well beaten by Australia. Like Ireland, they brought no points into the Super Eights. Unlike Ireland, however, they had won their first game in Guyana, beating Sri Lanka in the game in which Sri Lanka fast bowler Lasith Malinga had taken four wickets with successive deliveries.

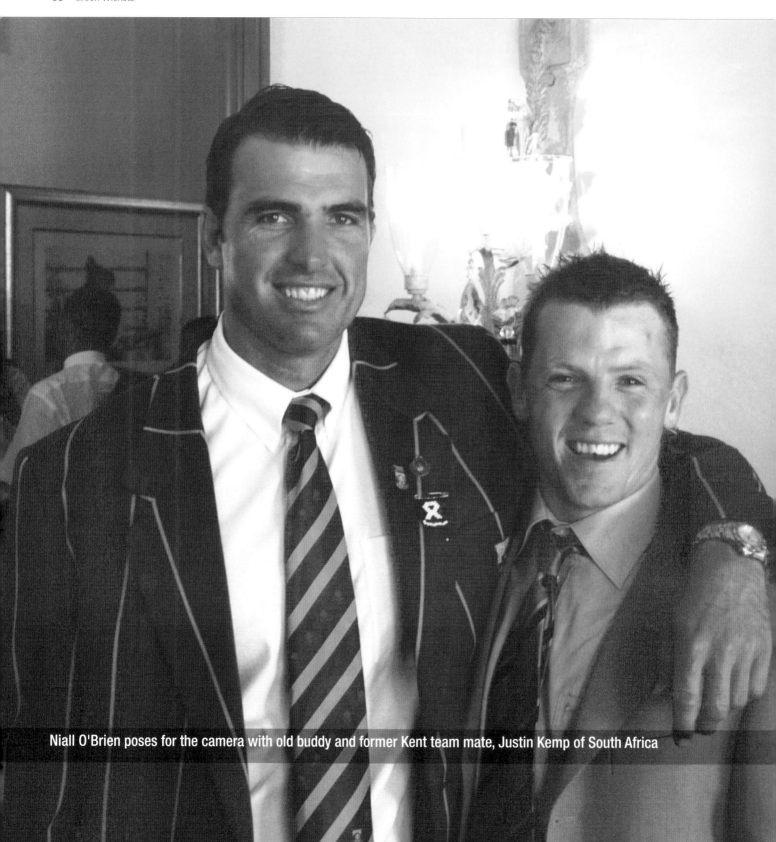

Niall O'Brien poses for the camera with old buddy and former Kent team mate, Justin Kemp of South Africa

Today's game was a special occasion for coach Adrian Birrell and all rounder André Botha, who were both coming up against the nation of their birth. Birrell knew the South African players well, while Botha had played alongside several members of the squad. Birrell believed that Ireland was being well supported back in South Africa, but that support was unlikely to continue for the Georgetown clash.

ADRIAN BIRRELL:

I've had a huge response; Port Elizabeth is going mad for Ireland. We trained there before the World League tournament and picked up a lot of supporters while we were there. Our confidence has certainly risen since we arrived in the Caribbean. We have a game plan and I believe that once we stick to it we will be competitive. Members of the other teams have being very supportive but we feel that some press reports have not given us the credit that is due. However, a good performance against South Africa can certainly enhance what we have done.

ANDRÉ BOTHA:

I don't think they were ready for the first game but I think they'll be much more prepared this time around. I know coach Mickey Arthur and Loots Bosman pretty well because I spent five years with them at Griqualand West, while I played with Charl Langeveldt and Roger Telemachus during my time with Boland. It's a great honour; every time I play against them the stage gets bigger, so the pressure to perform is growing.

The Irish knew that they would have to catch South Africa on an off-day and perform as they had done against Pakistan to have any chance of creating a shock in this Super Eights fixture. But they would go into this game as they had any other, and try to control the controllables and perform in all three disciplines. And the Irish captain was taking all the positives from the England game and intending to bring these into the South Africa clash while making sure that his team did not make the same mistakes again.

TRENT JOHNSTON:

We have to be a lot tighter in those last ten overs. We were there for the first forty against England but then gave up ninety runs, and you can't do that. It's difficult out there, sometimes you come up against quality players and if you're out a matter of inches the ball disappears. But if our opening bowling is good enough then I think we can restrict them to a decent total. We worked with some spin bowlers and with an open field, so we'll be looking to push ones and work the ball. We're looking at not getting squeezed in those middle overs.

South Africa had been given a scare against Ireland in the warm-up game but would have come into this fixture in Guyana confident of victory. Their coach, Micky Arthur, wasn't taking anything for granted, and said that they were targeting two of Ireland's bowlers and two batsmen whom they saw as a threat.

MICKY ARTHUR:

While we can look back on that game and say we approached it as just that, a warm-up game, this game is different. We are going there to get two points, and if it's a clinical performance, all the better. Ireland may be a team of amateurs, but they will always be tough, because they play for one another with a tremendous amount of passion.

The Proteas had class throughout, boasting some of the best batsmen in the world, in the form of Graeme Smith, Herschell Gibbs, A. B. de Villiers and Jacques Kallis, while their new-ball bowling attack, of Shaun Pollock and Makhaya Ntini, was as good as that of any side in the competition. However, it had rained every day since both teams had arrived, so there was a good chance that the game would be affected by inclement weather. Moreover, the wicket had been inadvertently flooded the day before the game. The toss would be crucial.

William Porterfield collides with South Africa's AB de Villiers

Sure enough, the rain arrived in force on the morning of the game, delaying the start by over an hour. To make matters worse, Ireland lost the toss and were put in to bat. Paul Mooney was named in the Ireland side, with Kevin O'Brien left out; otherwise, it was the same eleven who had lined up against England.

The game eventually got under way fifteen minutes after the scheduled 9.30 am start, and in the third over Ireland lost their opening wicket as Jeremy Bray was out for his second consecutive duck, trapped lbw off Pollock after facing nine balls on the slow and low Guyana pitch, which obviously wasn't to the left-hander's liking. Eoin Morgan and William Porterfield dug in and did well to survive the new ball, considering the strength of the bowling attack. Two rain delays later, the game had been reduced to a forty-seven-over match. Ireland resumed their innings on 19 for 1, in the tenth over. The scoreboard was suffering while the wickets were kept intact. After eleven overs, Ireland had notched up only twenty-three runs when, once again, rain stopped play. This time it looked as though the bad weather had come to stay.

Two hours later, the covers were off and play resumed, with the game now reduced to thirty-five overs. Considering the amount of rain that had fallen, the game would never have finished – and the teams would have shared the points – if they had been playing up the road at the old Bourda Stadium. With the sand-based outfield at the new stadium, however, shortly after the downpour had ended and the groundhog machines had done their job, play could restart. This was bad luck for Ireland considering their cautious approach to the new ball. With a little more than twenty overs remaining, the Irish had to change their approach and start scoring quickly. The revised total emphasised how important winning the toss was, and while it had gone in Ireland's favour against Pakistan, in this fixture it had given South Africa a huge advantage.

The thirteenth over was a productive one for Ireland, who scored eight from the six balls, but it also proved costly for them, as Porterfield, who had just played two terrific shots for six runs, played another ambitious shot and was brilliantly caught at point by Kallis, at full stretch running backwards,

leaving Ireland on 31 for 2. The only consolation for Ireland was that it was the end of Pollock's allocation: bowlers were allowed only seven overs each. Pollock's figures were superb (7–2–17–2), and Ntini (7–2–14–0) had also bowled well, although he had failed to take a wicket. Charl Langeveldt and Andrew Hall then came in to the attack. Niall O'Brien and Morgan put on a good stand of thirty-two off forty-four balls before Morgan was out for 28. It was a decent knock by the Middlesex batsman, but he gloved a short ball from Hall to give Ashwell Prince an easy catch. O'Brien was quickly into his stride, playing some big shots, including three boundaries, but his partnership with Andrew White, who came in at five rather than his usual seven – presumably after his impressive knock against England, or possibly to throw a right-hander into the attack to upset the bowling – lasted only seventeen balls, as the wicketkeeper was out after going after a ball down the leg side and clipping it to Herschelle Gibbs at point. It would probably have been a wide if O'Brien had left it but, on 25 from thirty-seven balls, O'Brien obviously felt he could score from the delivery.

White and new man in André Botha pushed the total past 100 in the twenty-seventh over, as Ireland's run rate approached a respectable four per over. The pair put on a very healthy 39 off thirty-six deliveries before White went for 30, hitting new bowler Graeme Smith's full toss to Gibbs at short-midwicket. White's strike rate was 100 – he had hit 30 off thirty balls – and with the score now up to 116 with six overs remaining, the Irish had a chance of posting a score in excess of 150 – a total which had looked highly unlikely when the Ireland run rate was below two per over. Captain Trent Johnston was next in, but Botha didn't hang around to build a partnership: he was caught by de Villiers at point after driving a delivery from Hall. Botha was out for 14 as McCallan joined Johnston in the middle. McCallan managed only three runs before departing in the next over after edging Langeveldt behind to wicketkeeper Mark Boucher, to leave Ireland on 124 for 7. Make that 124 for 8, as Paul Mooney was out first ball in a carbon copy of the dismissal his brother John had experienced against the West Indies. Mooney went after Langeveldt's short delivery down the leg side but gloved to Boucher, who took an easy catch. This was not a debut to remember for the Balrothery all-rounder, but in fairness to Mooney and McCallan, overs were running

The team enjoy a late-night barbeque at the Amakhala Game Reserve, where they spent a couple of days ahead of their warm-weather training in preparation for the World Cup

Ireland v. South Africa   Umpires: D J Harper, S J A Taufel

Ireland innings			runs	balls	4s	6s
J P Bray	lbw	b S M Pollock	0	9	0	0
W T S Porterfield	c J H Kallis	b S M Pollock	14	33	1	0
E J G Morgan	c A G Prince	b A J Hall	28	50	4	0
N J O'Brien	c H H Gibbs	b C K Langeveldt	25	37	3	0
A R White	c H H Gibbs	b G C Smith	30	30	5	0
A C Botha	c A B de Villiers	b A J Hall	14	20	0	0
D T Johnston	not out		13	14	0	1
W K McCallan	c M V Boucher	b C K Langeveldt	3	6	0	0
P J K Mooney	c M V Boucher	b C K Langeveldt	0	1	0	0
D Langford-Smith	not out		17	10	1	1
Extras		4w 1b 3lb	8			
Total		for 8	152	(35.0 ovs)		

Bowler	O	M	R	W	Fall of wicket	
S M Pollock	7.0	2	17	2	0	J P Bray
M Ntini	7.0	2	14	0	31	W T S Porterfield
C K Langeveldt	7.0	0	41	3	63	E J G Morgan
A J Hall	7.0	0	37	2	77	N J O'Brien
J M Kemp	3.0	0	14	0	116	A R White
J H Kallis	3.0	0	20	0	119	A C Botha
G C Smith	1.0	0	5	1	124	W K McCallan
					124	P J K Mooney

South Africa innings			runs	balls	4s	6s
A B de Villiers	c W T S Porterfield	b W B Rankin	0	3	0	0
G C Smith	c and b	D T Johnston	41	45	6	0
J H Kallis	not out		66	86	8	0
H H Gibbs	c A R White	b W B Rankin	6	15	1	0
A G Prince	not out		47	44	3	1
Extras		4nb 1w	5			
Total		for 3	165	(31.3 ovs)		

Bowler	O	M	R	W	Fall of wicket	
W B Rankin	7.0	1	26	2	1	A B de Villiers
D Langford-Smith	5.0	0	31	0	71	G C Smith
P J K Mooney	3.3	0	40	0	85	H H Gibbs
D T Johnston	3.0	0	15	1		
A C Botha	6.0	0	18	0		
W K McCallan	5.0	0	27	0		
A R White	2.0	0	8	0		

Kyle McCallan celebrates the wicket of Craig McMillan

Andrew White celebrates with captain Trent Johnston after taking the wicket of New Zealand's Daniel Vettori

The O'Brien brothers batting against the Black Caps, with Kevin hitting a magnificent 49 off 45 balls

Smith got in on the act, bowling well from the pavilion end, with new batsman Hamish Marshall going for 16 after slicing high and wide to Eoin Morgan, who made an excellent catch at cover, sparking the now-famous DLS 'Ferret' celebration, a unique dance routine that Langford-Smith performes for every wicket he takes. Despite the loss of wickets, New Zealand had pushed on to 59 for 2 off eleven overs, with Fulton seemingly able to deal with everything the Irish attack threw at him.

Langford-Smith struck again in the seventeenth over. Scott Styris edged a slower delivery to Niall O'Brien for an easy catch, and went for 10, leaving the Black Caps on 83 for 3. Langford-Smith completed his spell, bowling his tenth consecutive over, to finish with excellent figures of 10–1–41–2. Fulton eased past fifty, but the run rate slowed as spinners Kyle McCallan and Andrew White came into the attack. In the twenty-fifth over, McCallan was rewarded for his accuracy, with Craig McMillan going for 22 after mistiming his shot, and top-edging to Trent Johnston for an easy catch at gully. McCallan struck again in between rain breaks, trapping Stephen Fulton lbw for 83 in the thirty-ninth over; two overs later Jacob Oram went for 20, Morgan catching at long-off after the all-rounder didn't get hold of White's delivery. The Kiwis were 181 for 6 with less than ten overs remaining. The spin attack of McCallan and White had taken wickets and slowed the rate down to 4.5. If Ireland could keep the rate at that level, they would be in with a chance of taking another big scalp, and their first win of the Super Eights.

White took his second wicket when Daniel Vettori flicked one off his glove to the keeper for five. New Zealand were now struggling on 210 after forty-six overs; the Kiwis hadn't hit a boundary in the previous eleven overs. But then Brendon McCullum and James Franklin let loose for the final twenty-four balls, McCullum scoring 47 off thirty-seven balls before being caught on the boundary by Porterfield off Johnston in the final over. Franklin finished in style, not out on 34 from twenty-two balls, to post a final total of 263 for 8. Once more, the 'death' bowling had let Ireland down, and they would be looking at a required run rate of more than five an over – a tall order, given their penchant for a conservative approach to the opening ten overs of the innings.

The Irish lost their obligatory early wicket, Jeremy Bray edging Shane Bond to McCullum for one, before Morgan and Porterfield got a bit of rhythm going. But then Porterfield tried to launch a Bond delivery and was well-caught by Styris for 11, leaving Ireland on 22 for 2 after 7.2 overs. Morgan was next to go, caught behind for 15 in the thirteenth over off Jacob Oram's bowling. The required rate was already above six when Kevin O'Brien joined brother Niall at the crease. They proceeded to put a seventy-five-run partnership – fifty off sixty-eight balls – with Kevin playing some majestic shots, including three huge sixes and some fine drives. Niall was scoring slowly, giving Kevin the strike – an approach which was working well, even though the rate was now over seven. The younger of the brothers was giving a master class in batting against some of the best bowlers in the world, and reached 49 off forty-five balls. What happened next summed up Ireland's day. With Niall on strike, he appeared to call Kevin for a single but then sent him back; the all-rounder was well out of his ground, as Styris whipped the bails off the stumps to run him out one short of his maiden World Cup half-century. Surely any hopes of an Ireland victory disappeared with the run-out.

Three overs later, Niall followed his brother back to the pavilion as he attempted to slog-sweep Jeetan Patel's off-spin, but only found Jacob Oram at deep midwicket. Then the wickets started to fall, and the game was up for the Irish. First White, lbw for a duck, then Johnston for 13, again lbw, followed by Peter Gillespie for 2 – another Vettori lbw – and then McCallan, for another duck. Last to go was Rankin, Vettori trapping the big man lbw first ball. Ireland had lost their final seven wickets for twenty-four and were all out for 134 off 37.4 overs. New Zealand recorded an emphatic victory, by 129 runs.

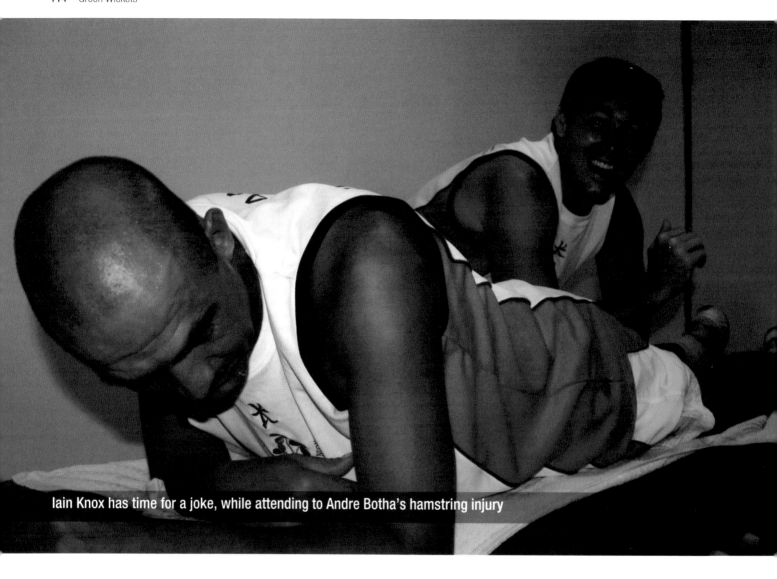

Iain Knox has time for a joke, while attending to Andre Botha's hamstring injury

TRENT JOHNSTON:

New Zealand are a special outfit. They are one of the favourites to win this thing, and there is no shame in losing to them, albeit heavily. When you consider the kind of bowling they [the O'Brien brothers] were up against, they really did well. While they were at the wicket, anything was possible. We were hoping that they could take us well into the fifty overs and see what happened from there. And our bowling and fielding were top again. Kyle McCallan and Andrew White were great again and we were restricting them at one point. And, like I say, our performance in the field is always good and we pride ourselves on it. So we'll take the positives out of this and try to learn from what went wrong.

KEVIN O'BRIEN:

You have to take a few positives from the game, with Kyle and Whitey bowling fantastically in the middle, and personally, I played probably the best innings that I have played since we went on tour. I tried to be a bit more aggressive in the nets during the week, and today there were a few bowlers that I targeted, the likes of [Scott] Styris, [James] Franklin and their off-spinner [Jeetan Patel], so once the ball was there I just hit it. TJ said in training to me to pick my ball and just hit it, and then pick up the singles as well, which I did pretty well, so 49 off forty-five balls was pretty pleasing.

ANDREW WHITE:

It was nice to tie them down there in the middle, but personal performances go out the window whenever you have a heavy defeat like that. They are a quality side and they played really well in the last five overs, to push their total on to 260 or so. That meant that we were behind the eight-ball from the start, and with Bond bowling well it pushed the run rate up above six an over, which meant it was very hard [for us], despite Kevin O'Brien batting really well at the moment. So there was no point just batting out the overs, we had to have a go. Although it was a heavy defeat, we went down fighting.

ADRIAN BIRRELL:

We have three opportunities left in the Super Eights, and if conditions go our way we will put up a good showing.

Kiwi skipper Stephen Fleming also admitted that his side had struggled at times during their innings.

STEPHEN FLEMING:

Up until forty overs, we felt we were behind. Ireland put pressure on us, and we weren't good enough to get partnerships through the middle. Today we were a little bit hesitant or over-aggressive, and what it did was create some pressure and anxiety as the batsmen went out, and Ireland capitalised on that. It wasn't until the last four or five overs that we stamped some authority on this game.

John Mooney celebrates with a well-deserved Banks beer or three

11   Barbados

After seventeen nights and three gruelling defeats at the Providence Stadium in Guyana, there was a spring in the step of every one of the Irish players as they boarded the plane at Cheddi Jagan International Airport for the short flight north to the idyllic island of Barbados. The team had three days to settle in to their new surroundings before they commenced what Adrian Birrell described as 'the most difficult game Irish cricket has ever played'. After two and a half weeks in Guyana, with very little to do – and even less when the rain fell, which was often – it was no surprise that arriving at the newly built five-star Hilton Hotel, complete with all mod cons and adjoining beach, would lift the spirits of this group of sportsmen, who had been on the road since January.

JEREMY BRAY:

I didn't go on any of the excursions [in Guyana], I probably watched about four million DVDs. Guyana was a difficult experience for me. The training facilities weren't great, and the pitches were pretty difficuly for me especially. I don't like the slow, low wickets, and I didn't score many runs there. I suppose coming up against world-class bowlers didn't help either. But there wasn't a whole lot to do, so it was the one part of the journey that I didn't really enjoy.

Walking around the Hilton would have reminded the team that they had reached the elite stage of the tournament: the majestic hotel was swarming with players from all the top teams, the match officials, and the ICC's top brass. Many of the players' friends and family members, who had missed out on the Guyana experience, were back in town, and this was another bonus for the squad.

ANDREW WHITE:

It's always nice to know when you're in a situation as intense as the World Cup that you have friends and family around you. You can turn your mind off from what went on at training the day before or what lies ahead. You can get your mind off the cricket, and that's been really important for a lot of the boys, as they had someone other than the team to turn too.

KYLE McCALLAN:

My Mam and Dad are very keen supporters and barely miss a cricket match that I play in, so it was massive for them [to be in the Caribbean], and my wife Lynne was out, and she had the benefit, once we qualified, of staying on for another three weeks. It's special having people that are close to you, because sometimes it's tough. Personally the Zimbabwe game was a tough experience for me. I didn't perform particularly well, and it's nice to have people around you, I suppose as a coping mechanismn to pick you up and drag you forward, and it worked very well and I'm exceptionally pleased to have had them out.

The team spent the day catching up with the other new arrivals and renewing their acquaintance with the sun at one of the hotel pools or down by the sea. Some of the players went out on jet-skis, while the golf enthusiasts got to play a round at the world-renowned Sandy Lane course. The restaurants of St Lawrence's Gap resort were a welcome distraction: the party atmosphere in the island's best-known resort was very much to the liking of the island's latest arrivals. The Digicel crowd had staged something of a reunion, with many jetting in from Jamaica, Guyana and Trinidad in the hope of reliving the earlier glory of Sabina Park. The party started in Mojo's Bar, and went on until the early hours at the Harbour Lights nightclub.

Barbados is the ideal cricket location, and it is little wonder that the Barbados Test always seems to generate the most travelling support in a series with the West Indies. At some games, you would think that the English were at home, as

Luckily John Boy packed the woolly hat for the Caribbean. The award winning new stand at the Kensington Cricket Ground in Barbados provides the awesome backdrop

thousands of Barmy Army enthusiasts would fill the ground – not to mention the many resorts dotted along the island's beautiful coastline.

The day before the Australia game, the team got to train at the recently developed Kensington Cricket Ground – one of the best-known cricket grounds in the world. The stadium was a sight to behold; thanks to a two-tiered temporary stand, the capacity was 28,000. The stadium paid homage to some of the great Bajans that have played for the West Indies: the three Ws – Frank Worrell, Everton Weekes and Clyde Walcott – Gordon Greenidge, Malcolm Marshall and Joel Garner, not forgetting the legendary Garfield Sobers, who was honoured at the stadium's entrance with a larger-than-life-size statue

The pitch, however, looked fast, and the Irish boys would need to be in top form to compete with the Aussies, the World Cup holders.

There was huge media interest in the Irish team ahead of their date with the world champions, and especially in the three Aussie-born players, Trent Johnston, Dave Langford-Smith and Jeremy Bray. The trio posed for the cameras and answered the same questions over and over about why they were playing for Ireland, and what it would be like for them to play against the country of their birth.

TRENT JOHNSTON:

I first played in Ireland twelve years ago, so I know the place and the people well at this stage. My wife's Irish; we're married eight years now. When Adi [Adrian Birrell] took over, we had a chat about getting a passport and coming back to play for Ireland.

JEREMY BRAY:

It gets a bit annoying when you see guys playing for other countries when they don't even live in the country. They just fly over and play for the country they wish to play for. People don't realise that I've been here for ten years, Trent [Johnston] has been here for six or seven, and Dave [Langford-Smith] for six, so I don't see why there should be a problem playing for your adopted country when you choose to live there. It gets a bit annoying but it's like water off a duck's back now. I've got two Irish-born kids, my wife is Irish, so I'm very much settled there. But that's not to say I won't move back to Australia one day [laughs].

Many of the original Blarney Army from Jamaica had returned to support the Ireland team for the remaining fixtures in Barbados and Grenada. Moreover, another batch of new arrivals had turned up, and with them came the stories of what things had been like back in Ireland during the group stages.

One of the main talking points was the celebrations that the Irish lads were engaging in after a wicket had been taken. Trent Johnston would celebrate with a chicken dance that had now become known worldwide as 'the Funky Chicken', while Dave Langford-Smith had a more unorthodox celebration, which he named 'the Ferret'. Even Kevin O'Brien had his one-legged shuffle, which first appeared in the Zimbabwe game, while there was also talk of a 'dolphin celebration', which was, thus far, yet to be unleashed. Banners were unveiled in the stadium to 'Do the Funky Chicken', and Langford-Smith was often accosted on the street or in the hotel lobby to perform the complex manoeuvre that was 'the Ferret'. He always obliged.

TRENT JOHNSTON:

Back when I first started going to nightclubs, my friends used to say that I danced like a chicken, so I thought it would be good fun to try and recreate it if I took a wicket at the World Cup. It's a bit of fun, and luckily it has come out on more than one occasion. Dave [Langford-Smith] has 'the Ferret', so I thought I'd better come up with something as well. I thought I'd try and send the funky chicken global and it looks like I have achieved it.

DAVID LANGFORD-SMITH:

OK, let's get this straight. 'The Ferret' is the original, and this stupid boc boc [mimics the 'Funky Chicken', what is that? It's rubbish. I brought 'the Ferret' out, and then he goes and copies me. It's ridiculous. Well, it's OK really [laughing]. But just so you know: which came first, the chicken or the ferret? 'The ferret' is the answer.

KEVIN O'BRIEN:

One of the lads back at Railway [Union], Greg O'Meara, always does the one-legged dance whenever we're out on the town, and he asked me to do it if I took a wicket at the World Cup. So when I took the wicket against Zimbabwe I did the dance for my buddy, who I knew would be watching back home. I think 'the Ferret' gets my vote, as it's an original dance. There are still a few more dances that haven't come out yet. There's a 'Duck' dance that Phil [Simmons] does, as well.

The team was split down the middle as to which celebration was the most popular.

JEREMY BRAY:

I suppose 'the Chicken'. But keep an eye out for 'the Dolphin'. It's something myself and Paul Mooney have been working on, so if I take a catch tomorrow, 'the Dolphin' will come out.

JOHN MOONEY:

I'm a big fan of 'the Funky Chicken'. It's more old-school, and I like that. 'The Ferret's good but 'the Funky Chicken' is better. There's talk about a 'Dolphin' coming out as well but the people behind 'the Dolphin' haven't taken a wicket or a catch yet, so that's why it hasn't turned up yet.

NIALL O'BRIEN:

It has to be 'the Ferret'. It's great. 'The Funky Chicken' is too common for me. 'The Ferret' has a bit of class.

KYLE McCALLAN:

It's hard between 'the Funky Chicken' and 'the Ferret'. It's a close one but I think I'd go for 'the Funky Chicken'. I could be cheeky and say we don't see it as much as we see 'the Ferret' – only joking – but it's something that the guys have brought to the team and the crowd have loved it. It's great to go around the stadium and see signs saying 'Do the Funky Chicken' or 'Show Us the Ferret'. The guys have made a name for themselves, and I think it's one of those thing that has endeared the Irish team to the public here, that we're out there giving it our all but we're really enjoying ourselves as well, so fair play to the two boys for taking it on.

IAIN KNOX:

I think they're both brilliant. We don't know which came first, 'the Ferret' or 'the Funky Chicken'. It's a tough call. But I'm going to go outside the playing team and say that the celebration with the most passion is when you're in the changing room and Adi Birrell watches a wicket go down, and he gives it the good old 'Yes please' and he runs out onto the balcony to clap and celebrate and then to watch either 'the Ferret' or 'the Chicken'.

ADRIAN BIRRELL:

A lot of the team spirit came down to the players themselves and the way they were led by Trent. I encouraged them to play with a smile on their face, but the way they did a jig after taking a wicket and the way they were enjoying themselves was down to the players. I'd go with 'the Ferret'. It's a unique dance that no one other than Dave Langford-Smith can do. Anyone can do 'the Funky Chicken', so I'll go with 'the Ferret'.

Aussie-born Ireland stars Trent Johnston, Jeremy Bray and Dave Langford-Smith share a drink following the Super Eights victory

12   Ireland v. Australia

A huge crowd swarmed into the stadium on the morning of the match. The Blarney Army was back in town, with lots of familiar faces back from Jamaica, and just as many new ones eager to be part of Ireland's World Cup adventure. And it wasn't just the Irish who were in town. Thousands of Aussies were swaggering into the Kensington Oval knowing that they should make light work of the Irish, while there was also an abundance of Indians and Pakistanis, who would have had this trip planned for a couple of years. The fact that their teams had gone home wasn't good enough reason for them to cancel a fantastic holiday to the Caribbean.

It may have had something to do with the Aussies being Ireland's opponents, but the Barmy Army was also in full effect – complete with Guinness hats, Ireland T-shirts and leprechaun suits – cheering on the Irish. The English fans were here for the cricket – and were hoping that Ireland could do what nobody had done to the Aussies since the 1996 final: beat them at the World Cup. But if South Africa, India, Pakistan, England and Sri Lanka couldn't beat the Aussies, what chance had the Irish?

TRENT JOHNSTON:

[The Australians] have been in pretty awesome form, so it's going to be a great occasion, and hopefully we can be competitive against them. This is the game that I've been looking forward to since we qualified for the Super Eights. It's great to get the opportunity to play against the guys that I grew up playing alongside and against. This is a huge occasion for the whole squad. It's a great occasion for me but it's also a great occasion for the other fourteen guys in the squad to play Australia at the World Cup.

ADRIAN BIRRELL:

This is the most difficult game that Irish cricket has ever played. But it's also a great challenge, and we can go in there and express ourselves and play the best we can. That's all we can do. But to play the best team in the world in this awesome stadium is really going to be an experience of a lifetime.

Irish captain Trent Johnston played six first-class games for New South Wales, and several of today's Australian squad were part of the same set-up, including Brad Haddin, Michael and Stuart Clarke, Nathan Bracken and Glenn McGrath – although Johnston never played in the same team as the Aussie bowling legend.

Over twelve thousand people had turned up to see the game. This showed that the Irish team were well supported: even if a few very high-profile names didn't want Ireland in the tournament, never mind the Super Eights, a lot of paying customers were voting with their feet to the contrary.

Australia captain Ricky Pointing won the toss. Instead of using the regulation overs to get some batting practice in, he chose to put Ireland in to bat, in the hope of getting them out early.

That's when the trouble began. Glenn McGrath took the new ball and was successful almost immediately, bowling Jeremy Bray for one with a fantastic yorker that smashed the off stump. William Porterfield also went for one, trapped lbw, beaten by the awesome pace of Shaun Tait. Tait was bowling at over 90 mph – a speed of bowling that few of the Irish players would have faced in domestic cricket. The new man in, Niall O'Brien, went for a duck on his first delivery, edging on to his stumps after going after a Tait wide. His brother Kevin came out to face Tait's hat-trick ball and survived, before resuming where he had left off in Guyana, hitting two early boundaries – and then taking a fierce smack from a Tait short ball for his trouble. Eoin Morgan managed to hang around for nine

Andrew White tries to gather himself after taking a fierce Glenn McGrath delivery on the helmet

balls but failed to score. McGrath's delivery had a bit of extra bounce, and Morgan edged to Matthew Hayden in the slips for an easy catch.

So with less than five overs gone, Ireland were in serious trouble at 12 for 4. This was what everybody had feared for Ireland coming into the World Cup: that they would be annihilated by one of the Test teams and would be shown up. Well if it's going to happen, it may as well be the Aussies who do it to you, and considering that this was Ireland's seventh game against Test-playing sides in the tournament so far, it wasn't anything to be ashamed about. But the Irish were probably not thinking this as they went in search of their first milestone – Canada's total of 36, which was the lowest score in World Cup history. The only thing going for Ireland at that stage was Tait's erratic bowling, which gifted them nine runs, from a combination of wides and no-balls.

Andrew White was greeted by a short ball to the head from McGrath in the ninth over. White took the hit full force and went down on his knees, before physio Iain Knox gave him the all-clear to remain on the pitch. Ireland pushed on to 32 for 4 before McGrath struck again. White, probably still dazed from the earlier strike, mistimed a slower ball, allowing Brad Hogg to take an impressive catch. Ireland, at 32 for 5 in the eleventh over, were still four shy of the dreaded record. Skipper Trent Johnston came out fighting and managed to smash ten off one McGrath over – and take Ireland past the Canadian score.

TRENT JOHNSTON:
I didn't even see the four balls Tait bowled at me. At least we put a score up. We're the ninth-worst score in World Cup history now. We were ticking off the scores when we were sitting in the dressing room, so that's one positive we can take from today.

O'Brien tried to follow his captain's example, but was out for 16 after clipping a Stuart Clarke delivery straight to Brad Hodge at midwicket. Kyle McCallan joined his captain at the crease and tried to steady the sinking ship. But it was the captain who went next. Having pushed on to 17, Johnston went after Tait's

bowling, but crashed an inside edge onto his stumps. Ireland were now in deep trouble on 56 for 7.

John Mooney made his second appearance of the tournament and quickly got off the mark with a couple of well-timed shots, which yielded five runs. Mooney continued to play some great shots, easing into double figures, while McCallan reached five before pushing an Andrew Symonds delivery to Tait at mid-on. Mooney was, by this stage, Ireland's top scorer on 19, but wasn't helped when Dave Langford-Smith went early in the twenty-fourth over, to leave Ireland on 80 for 9. Hogg's spin was too much for Langford-Smith, who flicked a tame shot to Ponting at short square-leg. Boyd Rankin came in and scored 4 as part of a forty-one-ball stand with Mooney. But the Ireland innings ended as the North County man, Mooney, was run out by Tait for 23, leaving Ireland on a lowly 91 all out after thirty overs.

It was still an hour to lunch as Australia came out to bat, with the unlikely opening partnership of Adam Gilchrist and Michael Hussey. They set about reaching the target in record time, with Gilchrist racing to 34 from twenty-five deliveries. The Irish captain will take very little from this game, but at least he will have the memory of watching Adam Gilchrist's middle and off stumps parting like the Red Sea as Johnston's in-swinging delivery flew inside the opener's drive, to give Ireland their first and only wicket of the game, in the ninth over. Andrew Symonds was next in for some batting practice, and within twenty-one balls the game was over, Hussey finishing it off with a huge six over midwicket. In the end, the Aussies won by nine wickets, with Hussey on 30 not out and Symonds unbeaten on 15.

TRENT JOHNSTON:
It's unfortunate. We set ourselves up to be really competitive today, but we were outclassed by the best team in the world. But it's pretty difficult when your top four batsmen score two runs between them. But that's the worst our top order has done since we arrived at the World Cup. We have played pace bowling well until today, so it's a positive that we can take.

ADRIAN BIRRELL:

We really struggled to bat against their [Australia's] bowlers. We survived against the [other Test sides] but didn't survive here. They looked a different class. It seems as if every team we come up against is better than the last. It was a gruelling experience to face that pace and consistency. McGrath has been the best bowler in the world for a long time and we struggled against him. Our top order got us into trouble and we never really got out of it. We're very disappointed, especially after the big crowd that turned up, but we were outclassed in the end. We are going to pick ourselves up. There is obviously bruising there that we need to get out of our system, but we've bounced back before and hopefully we can do it again.

JEREMY BRAY:

I played against quite a few of those players when I was younger, but it was a bit easier then than it is now. But it was great to meet up with a few old friends there and meet some people that I hadn't seen in a long time. And to play against them was huge, as they're just an unbelieveable unit these days.

KYLE McCALLAN:

When you start playing the game, you want to play the very best, and you dream of playing against the very best. The Australians play at a level that I have never experienced in eleven years of international cricket. They played the game so hard and fast and intensely, and maybe Irish cricket can learn from that.

RICKY PONTING:

The Irish boys would've been a bit nervous coming into the game. But when you've got McGrath and Tait bowling at their best on a new wicket with a new ball, it's always going to be hard. That could have happened to any team today that we knocked the top order over. But Ireland have been competitive in every game so far. Even in the game with New Zealand in the run chase, they weren't that far off the mark. A couple of wickets more in hand, and there might have been a chance there. That was a lot of the reason today for me bowling first, to get out there all guns blazing and try and knock over their top order, almost play them out of the game, rather than let them hang around in the game and be a nuisance, so that's what we did. But well done to the Irish guys and what they've achieved. They won their way into the Super Eights, they obviously won more games than India or Pakistan, and that's what the qualifying part of the tournament is for. I don't know a lot about Irish cricket. We've toured there a few times on Ashes tours but the games have been washed out with the rain. Now it's about them going home and growing the game back in Ireland.

TRENT JOHNSTON:

Growing up in Wollongong, I'd always gone to watch New South Wales or Australia play, and it was my dream to play for Australia, but it never happened. But I'm over that and I'm very lucky to have got the opportunity to play with Ireland, and to captain the team and play at the World Cup has been a huge honour and a huge thrill for me. And to play against the country you were born in and the country you support – other than Ireland – was a massive day [for me]. It was a disappointment that we didn't get to be competitive against Australia, as they are the powers of world cricket, and it would have been great to show them that Ireland as a cricket nation can play good cricket.

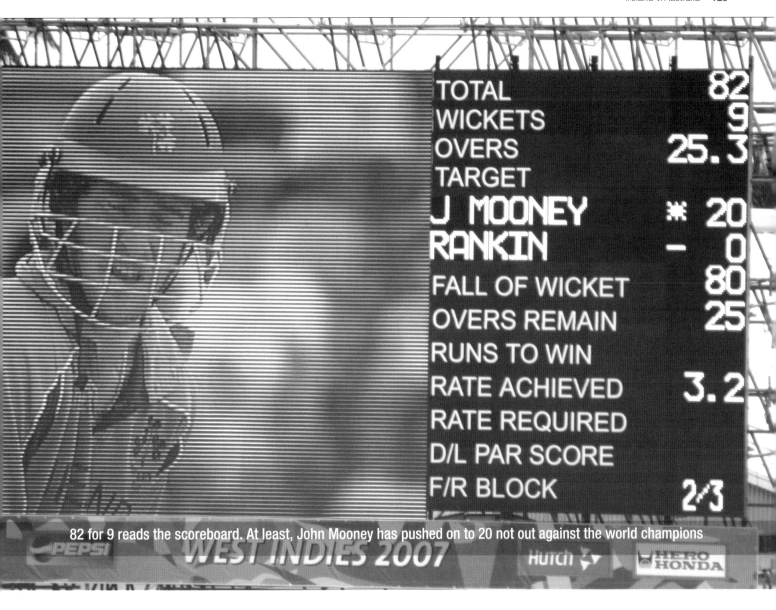

TOTAL		82
WICKETS		9
OVERS		25.3
TARGET		
J MOONEY	✳	20
RANKIN	–	0
FALL OF WICKET		80
OVERS REMAIN		25
RUNS TO WIN		
RATE ACHIEVED		3.2
RATE REQUIRED		
D/L PAR SCORE		
F/R BLOCK		2/3

82 for 9 reads the scoreboard. At least, John Mooney has pushed on to 20 not out against the world champions

The defeat by Australia was definitely a low point for the Ireland team, and a real knock to their confidence ahead of the most important game of the Super Eights: against Bangladesh two days later. It would take an awful lot of man-management and confidence-building to get the players ready for such an important clash. But anyone who knew Birrell and Johnston, or had got to know them over the Irish squad's epic journey through the Caribbean, would tell you that if anyone could pick up the pieces from this annihilation, they could.

Trent Johnston goes airborne to celebrate the wicket of Aussie legend Adam Gilchrist

Ireland v. Australia   Umpires: B F Bowden, R E Koertzen

Ireland innings			runs	balls	4s	6s
J P Bray		b G D McGrath	1	2	0	0
W T S Porterfield	lbw	b S W Tait	1	11	0	0
E J G Morgan	c M L Hayden	b G D McGrath	0	9	0	0
N J O'Brien		b S W Tait	0	1	0	0
K J O'Brien	c B J Hodge	b S R Clark	16	25	3	0
A R White	c G B Hogg	b G D McGrath	6	20	0	0
D T Johnston		b S W Tait	17	25	2	0
W K McCallan	c S W Tait	b A Symonds	5	18	0	0
J F Mooney	run out		23	44	2	0
D Langford-Smith	c R T Ponting	b G B Hogg	2	7	0	0
B Rankin	not out		4	19	0	0
Extras		1nb 15w	16			
Total		all out	91	(30.0 ovs)		

Bowler	O	M	R	W	Fall of wicket				
G D McGrath	7.0	1	17	3	2	J P Bray	54	D T Johnston
S W Tait	6.0	1	39	3	2	W T S Porterfield	72	W K McCallan
S R Clark	8.0	1	19	1	2	N J O'Brien	80	D Langford-Smith
G B Hogg	6.0	2	9	1	12	E J G Morgan	91	J F Mooney
A Symonds	3.0	1	7	1	32	A R White		
					42	K J O'Brien		

Australia innings			runs	balls	4s	6s
A C Gilchrist		b D T Johnston	34	25	4	0
M E K Hussey	not out		30	41	3	1
A Symonds	not out		15	9	1	1
Extras		1nb 8w 4lb	13			
Total		for 1	92	(12.2 ovs)		

Bowler	O	M	R	W	Fall of wicket	
D Langford-Smith	3.0	0	27	0	62	A C Gilchrist
W B Rankin	4.2	0	24	0		
D T Johnston	3.0	0	18	1		
J F Mooney	1.0	0	14	0		
W K McCallan	1.0	0	5	0		

Eoin Morgan learns an early lesson in the value of sun block while training at the University of Port Elizabeth ahead of four months in the sun

13   Ireland v. Bangladesh

It was billed as the game of the tournament. This was the only fixture other than the final and the semi-finals that had been sold out months in advance of the tournament commencing. The recently rebuilt Kensington Oval was chosen as the venue most suited to host such a high-profile game. Eventually the appointed day, Sunday 15 April, had arrived, and the eyes of the cricketing world tuned in for this highly anticipated clash. Ireland faced Bangladesh.

It was, of course, meant to be Pakistan versus India, the most high-profile cricket fixture in the world – no matter what the English and the Australians might tell you. A lot of the main sponsorship for the tournament was from Indian companies. In cricket magazines previewing the World Cup, the group games were often not listed, but if you looked at 15 April, it would say 'India v. Pakistan'.

(The top eight teams had been given a number to carry throughout the event. In Ireland's group, Pakistan were D1 and West Indies were D2; after Ireland went through rather than Pakistan, Ireland were D1 for the remainder of the tournament, despite the fact that the West Indies had won Group D. It was a similar story in Group B, where Bangladesh became B2 in place of India.)

The ICC now found themselves in a strange situation: they had sold all the tickets to the fixture, but there was a strong possibility that no one would turn up. They chose to open the gates free to the public from 11.00 am: they felt that anyone with a ticket would be well inside by then. A small number of Indian and Pakistani fans did turn up for the event, but they all entered the stadium with a look of melancholy on their faces – they felt they had been let down by their respective sides. The Blarney Army was again there in force, as was the Barmy Army, which once more turned up to support the boys in green. The Indian and Pakistani fans didn't take long to get over their state of protest, as they joined in to create the best atmosphere of the tournament so far, except for possibly the opening fixture, when the West Indies fans were in top form.

The Indians supported the Irish, as Ireland had knocked out their great rivals, Pakistan: this also made sense as the flags of both nations contained the same three colours. Pakistan fans were in the minority, and it made sense that they supported Bangladesh, who had beaten India. To be fair to both sets of fans, though, they just added to the atmosphere and acknowledged and applauded good cricket.

The fixture was also targeted by the Irish as the Super Eights game that they would have the most realistic chance of winning. But going into the game, Ireland were underdogs, considering that Bangladesh had already beaten South Africa in the Super Eights and made England work hard for their victory. And Bangladesh had beaten India in the group stages, so they were by no means a pushover. Bangladesh had three spinners in their line-up, and people were predicting that the Irish, who had struggled with good spin throughout the tournament, would come unstuck here. Ireland did receive a boost of sorts before the game as England batsman Kevin Pietersen addressed the team and spoke extensively on the best way to play Bangladesh's spin attack. The adopted Englishman had recently been named as the top one-day-international batsman in the world, so the Irish would have welcomed his advice (even though Pietersen had been undone by the left-arm spin of Abdur Razzak for ten runs in their recent encounter).

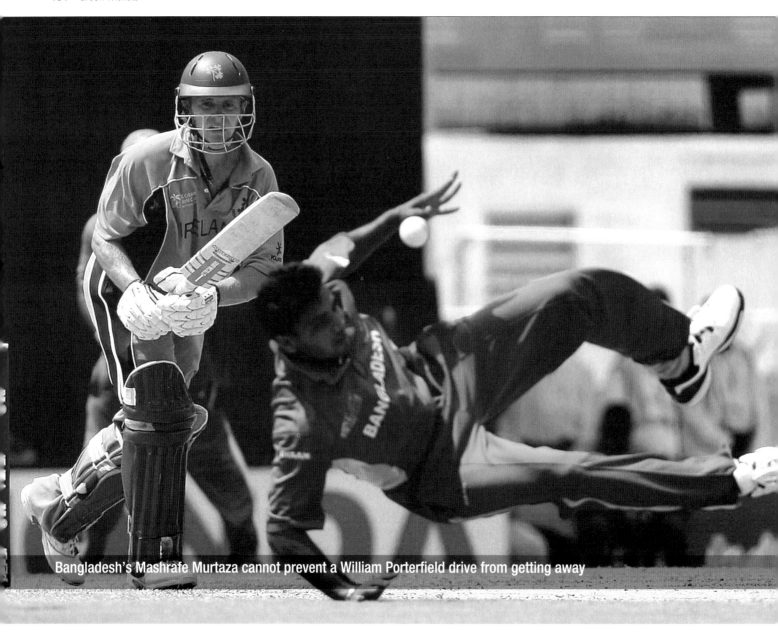

Bangladesh's Mashrafe Murtaza cannot prevent a William Porterfield drive from getting away

The sun was shining as usual in Bridgetown ahead of the game, and while conditions were perfect for cricket, one would have thought, judging by the bouncy pitch, that whoever won the toss would bowl first. André Botha was back in the side after missing two games with a hamstring injury, which meant that John Mooney, Ireland's only player to perform against Australia, was relegated to twelfth man. Trent Johnston won the toss for Ireland but obviously had a game plan in mind, and decided to bat first. Enter Porterfield and Bray.

The Bangladesh opening bowlers, Shahadat Hossain and Marhrafee Bin Mortaza, didn't cause Jeremy Bray or William Porterfield too much trouble in the early overs, and Ireland advanced to 23 for no loss after six overs. Remarkably, this was Ireland's highest opening stand by a long distance at the World Cup: the previous highest had been seven against Pakistan. Porterfield looked relaxed and confident as he pushed on past thirty; Bray started slowly, but both openers were quite happy with the partnership. Bangladesh brought on their first spinner, Abdur Razzak, after twelve overs but he caused no immediate problems, and Ireland scored five off the over. There were around a thousand Irish supporters spread throughout the sizeable crowd – although it looked like there were many more, thanks to the green, white and orange flags of the large Indian contingent.

Ireland lost their first wicket in the twenty-sixth over. Bray was run out for 31 as Porterfield looked for a quick single to get to his half-century. The opening partnership had reached a substantial 92, and although it hadn't come in record time, it left Ireland with a full complement of batsmen, minus Bray, to push on for the remaining twenty-four overs. Eoin Morgan was almost out on his second delivery, smashing the ball over midwicket, but he was dropped by Shahadat close to the boundary, with the ball crossing the rope for four. Porterfield did get his first fifty of the World Cup a few minutes later, as Ireland tried to increase the run rate, and they reached 100 in the twenty-eighth over. Bangladesh struck again late in the same over. Morgan was chasing a second run, but some excellent fielding led to him being run out for five.

Niall O'Brien came in next, and scored a quick-fire ten before being caught by substitute Farhad Reza off Tamim Iqbal Khan. O'Brien had tried his trademark reverse-sweep, but Farhad was waiting in the gully, and took an easy catch. Kevin O'Brien was next in, and promptly hit a four, and then a huge six, which crashed off the top of the pavilion, helping Ireland push on to 160 for 3 after thirty-nine overs, the run rate edging just over four. Porterfield continued to impress, moving on to 85, while O'Brien was already on 28, from twenty-four balls.

Porterfield walked in the forty-second over. Mortaza's delivery was skied by the Ulsterman, giving Rafique an easy catch at short fine leg. The skipper, Johnston, came out to join O'Brien, and wasted no time getting into double figures, while O'Brien smashed another six high into the Malcolm Marshall end. In the forty-eighth over, O'Brien was run out, again, just short of his half-century. The skipper called for a second but O'Brien didn't make it in, after some excellent glove-work from Mushfiqur Rahim. Andrew White was next in but was run out for three, trying to snatch a second run that wasn't there. In the last over, Johnston was caught by Shahriar Nafees, again off Mortaza's bowling, the captain once more impressing with the bat, scoring 30 off twenty-three balls. Dave Langford-Smith, 6, and André Botha, 1, finished the innings off, leaving Ireland on the impressive total of 243 for 7 after fifty overs.

JEREMY BRAY:

The Bangladesh bowlers didn't bowl me any width and kept it very straight, but they kept the same plan with Porty [William Porterfield], who loves it like that, so he was scoring at one end and I was just hanging in there at the other. But I still managed to tick over a bit. It shows what can happen when you get off to a good start, and it's just a pity we didn't do it more often in the World Cup. But having said that, we've been coming up against world-class bowlers who we're not used to facing, but I'm sure if we'd got off to a good start in one or two of the games, maybe against England or New Zealand, we could have won at least one or two of those games.

A local Bajan gets behind the 'boys in green' at the Ireland versus Bangladesh game in Barbados

Bangladesh started their innings slowly. Boyd Rankin struck the first blow, in the seventh over, with Shahriar Nafees attempting to hook the big man, and giving keeper O'Brien an easy catch. Bangladesh increased the rate but lost another wicket in the eleventh over, as Botha's first delivery was nicked by Aftab Ahmed to O'Brien. Botha's lightning reflexes gave Ireland their third wicket in the thirteenth over, when he touched Tamin Iqbal's straight drive on to Saqib Al Hasan's stumps. Hasan was run out for three, and Bangladesh were on 48 for 3. Mohammad Ashraful and Iqbal built a good partnership, but Iqbal then chopped at a Johnston yorker and clipped the ball on to his stumps. Iqbal was out for 29, leaving Bangladesh on 93 for 4. Ashraful followed in the twenty-second over, hooking Rankin to Langford-Smith, and was out for 35. Rahim was next to go, bowled by Kyle McCallan for 16, and Langford-Smith caught and bowled Mortaza for a duck. McCallan and Johnston finished the Bangladesh innings off, taking Razzak and Bashar respectively, as Ireland won comfortably, by seventy-four runs, with opener Porterfield scooping the man of the match award for his great knock of 85.

The large crowd showed their appreciation for a truly great game of cricket as the Irish team enjoyed their deserved lap of honour. This was Ireland's World Cup final, and they won it in style, performing in all three disciplines. This must have been extremely satisfying for Ireland coach Adrian Birrell. The win pushed Ireland into seventh in the Super Eights table but, more importantly, by beating a second Test nation, Ireland secured full one-day-international status. The victory seemed as important – if not more important – to the players and management as the Pakistan result had. It was a great game of cricket, with a high-quality performance from the Irish, and represented the perfect lift after some tough encounters against the best teams in the world.

TRENT JOHNSTON:

I thought they [Porterfield and Bray] were outstanding – they really set the foundations for our win. I can't give those guys enough credit for what they did out there. We spoke about it after the game. We knew we had to get all three disciplines right today, and I think we did that. The way the Bangladesh spinners were bowling, the last thing we wanted to do was chase 220 to 230 on that particular wicket. So we made a decision that we were going to go out there and bat first and try to put a competitive score on the board, which we did. When we bowled, we hoped we could squeeze them, with big Boyd Rankin and David Langford-Smith, and I thought they bowled fantastically well. And coming back two days after we were blown off the park by Australia, to beat Bangladesh was a huge effort from the guys and was probably the best one-day performance that I have been involved with since I started playing for Ireland. It was the best complete performance; we put all batting, bowling and fielding disciplines together on the one day in a massive arena in a massive game.

WILLIAM PORTERFIELD:

We weren't too disappointed to bat first – we were looking forward to it. We knew there was going to be a bit of pace and bounce, but we managed to get past that and set a good total. We got stuck to start with. It wasn't easy, but we dug in, and managed to come through the early spell, and thankfully we got a few runs.

ANDREW WHITE:

I'll never forget Barbados, even though we were only there for six days. The Kensington Oval and Barbados is steeped in so much cricketing history, and when you stand out there in the middle of the ground and look around at how many of the stands are named after so many great cricket players... you just realise that you are in the real centre of cricketing history, and thankfully we made our own wee bit of history from a World Cup point of view [by beating Bangladesh].

SHAHADAT – 0
FALL OF WICKET 169
OVERS REMAIN 9
RUNS TO WIN
RATE ACHIEVED 4.1
RATE REQUIRED
D/L PAR SCORE 187
F/R BLOCK 3/3

WEST INDIES 2007

Adrian Birrell joins his team to celebrate on the pitch after beating Bangladesh

The team bus rolled into the car park of the Hilton Hotel a couple of hours later. The echo of the underground car park made the accompanying rendition of 'Ireland's Call' all the louder. One by one the team descended, some still singing, others drinking bottles of Banks beer as they made their way into the hotel. The open-air, beachfront bar was the perfect place to unwind after such a performance on the field, and while many would have expected that a crazy last night in Barbados was on the cards, it ended up being a civilised affair, with all the team members relaxing in the hotel bar amongst family and friends. Having everyone together after such an important victory seemed like the perfect end to an amazing day.

Niall O'Brien in touch-rugby action for the Youngies

14 Homeward Bound: Grenada

The atmosphere on the flight from Barbados to Grenada could only be described as giddy. The team laughed and joked their way through the hour-long flight to their final destination, the island of Grenada. Again there was a welcome party for the Irish boys, this time by a group of drummers and a colourful dance troupe. The team probably reached their hotel before their bags were off the plane, as the Rex Resort was less than five minutes away – two if you've got a police escort.

The complex sprawls over several acres, running down to the secluded beaches and the majestic ocean. The swimming pool is up on a height overlooking the sea, although it is a bit of a stroll from the main hotel – a small price to pay for luxury. There is also an in-house chauffeur, complete with golf buggy, to ferry you around at your leisure.

The Queen's Park stadium is in the town of St George's, about ten kilometres from the hotel, and was another one of the Caribbean stadia that had been refurbished. As with the rest of the island, the original stadium was badly damaged during Hurricane Ivan in 2004; the wrecked football stadium, still sitting beside the new cricket ground, is a reminder of how badly the island was hit by the hurricane. Several hotels have been rebuilt since the storm, and as a result, the resort of Grand Anse, which sits halfway between the Ireland team hotel and the stadium, boasts some of the best hotels in the Caribbean. Again Digicel came up trumps for phones and hotels for some of the media, while a tour of the main resort was also organised.

Just like Barbados, Grenada is the type of place you could see yourself coming back to in a heartbeat. It was paradise. While the players had several days booked to relax after the Sri Lanka game, the remaining media were booked to go home the day after the game – if the reserve day was used, there'd be a few problems for the last of the Irish press 'puddle'. Only three Irish media personnel had stayed in the Caribbean for the duration of the World Cup: RTÉ's John Kenny; Paul Davey, a Sligo man who was making a documentary; and yours truly. It was a long sojourn in the Caribbean, but a week doing nothing in a place like Grenada would have been the perfect way to unwind. It wasn't to be.

There was one piece of unfinished business for the team to sort out before the final game of the Super Eights. A game of touch rugby had been incorporated into the training regime to help with the players' fitness levels; over the course of the previous four months, it had turned into a pretty competitive event. The squad was spilt according to age, with Andrew White as the cut-off point. White and those older than him were imaginatively called the 'Oldies', and all those who were younger than him were part of the 'Youngies'. Physio Iain Knox was the referee, and was pleasantly surprised by how seriously the lads were taking the fixture.

IAIN KNOX:

It all started when we left in January. We knew we'd be away for three months and that I'd be doing a lot of fitness with them, so the last thing the guys wanted to hear is that they have to run so many laps, or up hills. Initially it was three teams – 'Roy's Rhinos', 'Birrell's Buffaloes' and 'Knoxie's Kudus' – but then it became two when we split it into the 'Youngies' and the 'Oldies'. The guys didn't realise that they were working so hard as they were just trying to beat each other, and that's why it has worked so well. And I'm sorry to say, but it is very much more competitive than the cricket we play at the World Cup. You know there's a lot at stake, a lot of bragging rights. The Youngies won Trinidad, then the Oldies won Jamaica and Guyana, and the Youngies squared it in Barbados, so we had to settle it in Grenada, and the Oldies took the Grand Final 5–2, to take the 'Snip Snip Trophy'. No matter what happens, I'm a loser for half the team, and I get a lot of abuse from the losing side. But it keeps them running around. We put a lot of emphasis on our fitness and being one of the fittest and best-fielding sides in the World Cup. And we play lots of different sports. We play rugby, Gaelic football and soccer, just to keep the guys running, doing lots of fast foot-work and sprint drills. It's all incorporated in all these different sports, and that shows on the cricket pitch.

The Oldies pose after winning the Snip Snip trophy

Arriving in Grenada, the series was tied, which meant that the final training session at the stadium would decide the outright winners. It was a heated affair, with experience just edging it, to give the title to the Oldies. The trophy was presented to captain Dave Langford-Smith, and the team celebrated with a lap of honour at the almost-empty stadium – much to the amusement of the onlooking media and stadium staff.

KYLE McCALLAN:

It's very competitive with all these whippersnappers. You know, when I was new to the squad, I wouldn't have said boo to a goose. They [the Youngies] are quite a confident bunch of boys, so it's always nice to take them down a peg or two. And today was the icing on the cake. I think Knoxie fixed it so that it would go right until the last day, but the cream is always rising to the top, and the performance of the Oldies today in the final of the touch rugby was just sensational, and we put the Youngies firmly back in their place.

DAVE LANGFORD-SMITH:

The golden Oldies won the rugby, and we're on cloud nine, and we've got another four or five days to give the youngsters loads of abuse.

JEREMY BRAY:

The Oldies will always win it, no problem. They've got me in the team. It had been a long road, and despite spending the last few days in tropical paradise, the players were also thinking of home and starting the next chapter of their remarkable cricketing careers. They've got me in the team.

It had been a long road, and despite spending the last few days in tropical paradise, the players were also thinking of home and starting the next chapter of their remarkable cricketing careers.

KYLE McCALLAN:

A lot of the stuff I've been hearing is hard to take in and hard to believe. The kids are all playing in the street, and record numbers are attending Easter camps. We've heard about the impact of what we've achieved back home, and I'm looking forward to getting home, and hopefully if we finish on a big high we'll go home to experience the acclaim that this squad deserves for where we've taken Irish cricket.

JEREMY BRAY:

It'll be nice to get home to Ireland. The body needs a bit of a rest, even though it's not going to get much. But I am looking forward to getting home and seeing friends, even though it has been a fantastic trip. It will be nice to get back to Ireland, but then, I suppose, after a week back home I'll be looking to get going again, or get back here again.

ANDREW WHITE:

It's coming to the end now. A lot of the guys are ready to go home. The supporters have been out, and family have been out, but they're all home now. It would be nice to go home now and relive a bit of the World Cup experience elsewhere, you know, watching a bit of it on TV and reading the papers, the stuff we've missed out on, having been away for so long, but you wouldn't have changed that for the world. The boys have been very level-headed throughout the tournament and dealt with everything in a professional manner. I think it's now time to go home and enjoy what has been a special occasion for us and share the memories with everyone else back home. And behind every set of Irish eyes there's a thousand stories, so there'll be plenty of those told.

Eoin Morgan, Dave Langford-Smith, Kevin O'Brien, William Porterfield and John Mooney relax by the pool in Grenada after the Sri Lanka match

15   Ireland v. Sri Lanka

Four countries, five weeks and eight games since making their World Cup debut in Sabina Park against Zimbabwe, Ireland faced the in-form Sri Lanka at the National Stadium in Grenada, in their final game of the Super Eights, and their curtain call at the 2007 Cricket World Cup. It was a flying visit to the southern Caribbean nation, as the Irish arrived on Monday and trained at the stadium on the Tuesday, and the game was played on Wednesday. With their opponents looking relaxed and confident, having safely negotiated their way to one of the four semi-final berths, the Irish – although, as always, in good spirits – were about to play their fourth game in ten days and must have been running on empty. With a long season back home about to start, the Irish team must have been looking forward to getting this game out of the way and then enjoying the few days' break that they had to look forward to once the small matter of being competitive with Sri Lanka had been taken care of.

And while the future looked promising for Irish cricket, the Sri Lanka game signalled the end of coach Adrian Birrell's tenure, as he was stepping down after five years in the hot seat. It had been a fantastic voyage for Birrell, and surely, as the last day at the office had arrived, his emotions would have been running high. Birrell is a self-confessed emotional man, and if he was trying to hide the emotions before his final game in charge, he was – for once – doing a bad job.

ADRIAN BIRRELL:

It's my last day at the office and it's going to be a pretty emotional day for me. But the guys will do their utmost and hopefully we'll play well. The last five years have been unbelievable and I'm leaving the job a very satisfied and proud man. I've been a team coach for over twenty years and this team is very special. I think when I look back at this team, as great as the performances have been, I'm as proud of the way that they are playing their cricket and how the fans here have taken to them. And not just here, but from all around the world I'm getting word back of how people are enjoying the way that we are playing the game.

I'm especially pleased with our fielding and the way the lads have battled for me, for the team and for the cause. We put in the hard work there and had a strategy that it would be a major factor in our success, and it has proven so. There are four guys who played in my first match against Notts [Nottinghamshire] in 2002. Kyle McCallan, Paul Mooney, Peter Gillespie and Andrew White, they've gone the full journey with me. And while no one player is any more special than the others, I suppose that those guys that have been with me the longest will always have a special part in my memories. I'm pretty confident that the future of Irish cricket is in good hands. The CEO [Warren Deutrom] and the new coach [Phil Simmons] will take Irish cricket to even greater heights.

And while Birrell's legacy was already secure before the tournament commenced, he knew that Ireland's adventure at the World Cup in the Caribbean would be remembered fondly, not only in Ireland but throughout the cricket-playing world, where the Irish story has been followed with huge interest.

John Mooney signals to the photographer [his brother Paul] that only two overs are remaining

ADRIAN BIRRELL:

This World Cup, and this Irish team, will always be remembered in Irish cricket's history, and it's important for me that I was part of it and in some way was an architect in the building of this team. It's very, very satisfying knowing that I've done some good. It would have been a little bit hollow had we not had a victory in the Super Eights, but that victory against Bangladesh was very special, as we really performed well on the day, playing a great brand of cricket. We had to, because they are a very good side.

Going into the Sri Lanka game, fourteen out of the fifteen players in the squad had played at least one match, and any changes to the side so far – apart from Kevin O'Brien's omission against South Africa – had been injury-related. Kenny Carroll was the only player yet to take part in the World Cup, although he was twelfth man against New Zealand, so he had spent plenty of time in the field, not to mention the endless running for drinks, gloves, bats and helmets. And judging by the way Kenny was grinning like a Cheshire cat in the team hotel the night before the game, it was clear that he was going to make his dream debut.

It was an injury to Andrew White that had propelled Carroll into the team, which was otherwise unchanged from the eleven that had beaten Bangladesh. The Irish captain was asked earlier in the tournament whether he should practise his tossing – cue giggles from the assembled media – as he had a habit of losing the pre-match ritual. Well, if he *had* been practicing, it must have been luck that was against him, as Sri Lanka won the toss. Following Ricky Ponting's example, they chose not to use the game as a glorified nets session, and put Ireland in to bat first. In a roundabout way, this was a compliment to the Irish team, as Ponting had said that he thought Ireland could be a nuisance – if not a threat; Mahela Jayawardene must had thought something similar as he set about trying to knock over Ireland's top order.

A decent crowd of just over seven thousand turned up to watch the game at the recently rebuilt stadium. There was a large Irish contingent – although not as many as had turned up for the Barbados games – and a fair smattering of Sri Lankans, mostly sporting Lasith Malinga novelty wigs. (These people were to be disappointed, as Malinga hadn't recovered from injury, and missed the game.) The Party Stand was unusually silent in the early part of the match: most of the occupants were using the giant scoreboard's shadow as relief from the searing sunshine. It was another scorcher in the field, and the track was flat and hard, which would suit the batting in the first innings. The Irish had a chance to post a decent total and put some pressure on with the bowling later on. Things started well for the Irish as Porterfield and Bray easily negotiated the opening overs – and, for only for the second time in the tournament, took their opening partnership into double figures. Things were moving along nicely – if a little slowly – until the eighth over, when Bray decided to open his shoulders, with Ireland on 20 without loss. Things weren't going to plan for Jayawardene – the Aussies had had Ireland at 12 for 4 in half the time – and they got worse as Bray let loose, driving successive boundaries off Farveez Maharoof. The fact that the same bowler turned out to be man of the match says a lot about what was about to happen in Grenada.

Maharoof's next delivery got rid of Bray as he spooned one to cover, where Russel Arnold took a fantastic tumbling catch. That was the start of the madness. André Botha was elevated to bat at three but could only edge behind for a duck two balls later. Eoin Morgan followed, edging to Kumar Sangakkara with the next ball for Maharoof's third wicket of the over. Niall O'Brien was next in, with Ireland under pressure on 28 for 3. Porterfield had held on while wickets were being lost all around him, but after patiently moving on to 17 from fifty-one balls, Maharoof struck again: Porterfield attempted to play a straight drive but managed only to loft one to Sanath Jayasuriya at mid-on, to leave Ireland in big trouble on 46 for 4 after eighteen overs.

Porterfield's was the first of three more Irish wickets to fall in a six-ball spell, thanks to a change in bowling that saw spin legend Muttiah Muralitharan come into the attack.

A champagne-soaked Adrian Birrell and all-rounder Paul Mooney bow out of Irish cricket after fifteen years combined service to the country

The 'smiling assassin' took a wicket with his second ball, Niall O'Brien edging to Sangakkara, O'Brien out for four, and two balls later Carroll was bowled around his legs as he attempted a sweep shot. Ireland were in big trouble on 48 for 6 after nineteen overs.

Things got worse. Trent Johnston lasted less than an over, before being run out by Maharoof for a duck. The captain was outside the crease after playing a tame shot, and the bowler reacted quickly, hitting the stumps thanks to a deflection off the skipper's foot, before Johnston could get back into his ground. With only twenty overs gone, Muralitharan made it 49 for 8 when Kevin O'Brien top-edged a weak shot to Jayasuriya for an easy catch. O'Brien was out for 2, making it five wickets lost for only three runs.

Langford-Smith came out and hit some nice shots but Murali struck again in the twenty-third over, trapping new man in Kyle McCallan lbw for a duck. Ireland were down and out on 54 for 9. Boyd Rankin was last man in and it was only 11.15 am. Langford-Smith at least gave the sparse crowd something to cheer about when he smashed Maharoof into the stand for six. The opening bowler then survived a very close stumping before smashing another boundary, to move on to 16 off fourteen balls. Chaminda Vaas took the final wicket, Langford-Smith missing a full toss. The umpire had no hesitation in giving the lbw, and Ireland were all out for a miserable 77, the sixth-lowest score in World Cup history. Rankin finished unbeaten on 7 off seventeen balls, including a well-taken boundary off Muralitharan's bowling – one for the grandkids, as they say.

After a quick turnaround, Ireland came out to bowl, with Rankin and Langford-Smith taking the new ball. They started well, with Rankin dismissing Upul Tharanga for a duck in the first over, thanks to a fine catch by William Porterfield at gully. Langford-Smith took the second wicket, in the fourth over. Sangakkara attempted to smash the ball square to the offside boundary but Carroll dived low to his left to take a tremendous catch at cover – and make up for his disappointing duck on his tournament debut. But that's where the World Cup story ended for Ireland, as Jayasuriya and Jayawardena finished things off, scoring 24 and 39 respectively as Sri Lanka hit 81 for

2 and took the game by eight wickets with forty overs to spare. Again, lunch would be served after the crowd had gone home.

The post-match press conference was the last time that Adrian Birrell would address the media as Ireland coach, and while he was clearly disappointed with the way the game had played out, he knew that he could be really proud of the bigger picture. His captain joined him at the top table as they bade farewell to the world press, who had been hanging on to their every word for the past six weeks as the Irish fairy tale was being written.

ADRIAN BIRRELL:

I'm feeling a bit disappointed with our performance today. We would have hoped to have put up a better show. Having lost some wickets, we came unstuck against Muralitharan, but we won't be the last team to do that. I always feared the Australia and Sri Lanka games, as we never face that type of bowling, and everyone in world cricket knows the difficulties there are when you face unique bowling. It was very difficult to face Tait and McGrath, as it was the worst type of wicket to play Australia on. I'm sure we would have done better on another type of wicket, and Sri Lanka was always going to be tough. I was always worried about Muralitharan, as we have never faced him, and fortunately Malinga didn't play. But then I didn't think Maharoof was a problem, and he got three wickets in one over. But I'm looking at my stint with Irish cricket over five years, and not just one match, and I'm very satisfied that I'm passing the baton over in better shape than when I received it. We've moved it forward and there is a great bunch of players now who are well placed to take the game even further, and I'm very proud of that.

TRENT JOHNSTON:

The disappointing thing is that we're sending him [Birrell] off with a bad result. But he knows that we went out there and did our very best. This tournament, and especially this Super Eights campaign, was something that we wanted to dedicate to him for what he's done for us and what he's done for Irish cricket.

Ireland's final wicket of the World Cup: The team congratulate Kenny Carroll after his superb catch

Dave Langford Smith and Boyd Rankin at the conclusion of the Ireland innings versus Sri Lanka

So, having faced the media for the last time, there was a far more difficult challenge waiting upstairs in the Ireland dressing room. The team would have to be addressed, and farewell speeches needed to be delivered. Only then could the after-party officially begin. A few well-deserved crates of Banks beer, as well as several bottles of champagne, were on ice while the team were grabbing a quick bite to eat and catching up on their lost fluids as they recovered from another gruelling – albeit shortened – day in the Caribbean sunshine.

Birrell spoke first, thanking the players for their efforts and for his experiences over the past five years. It was emotional stuff and was finished of by a champagne shower that drenched the departing supremo. The captain also thanked everyone for their efforts, with a special mention for the boss. He also announced Paul Mooney's retirement from the international game after ten years wearing the green shirt.

PAUL MOONEY:

I got to represent my country for ten years, and all my ambitions and hopes for Irish cricket have been realised. We qualified for our first World Cup, just played in it and did really well, and hopefully we have promoted the game to everyone back in Ireland. One of the goals that I had set was that hopefully by the time I finished my career, Irish cricket would be on the up and that people would start to recognise this great sport for what it is. I'm going out at the top. It doesn't get any better than this.

The party kicked in soon afterwards, with a stirring rendition of the team's adopted anthem, 'Ireland's Call'.

The party continued back by the hotel swimming pool bar as the sun set in Grenada – and on Ireland's World Cup adventure.

Ireland v. Sri Lanka   Umpires: M R Benson, B R Doctrove

Pakistan innings			runs	balls	4s	6s
J P Bray	c R P Arnold	b M F Maharoof	20	29	4	0
W T S Porterfield	c S T Jayasuriya	b M F Maharoof	17	51	1	0
A C Botha	c K C Sangakkara	b M F Maharoof	0	2	0	0
E J G Morgan	c K C Sangakkara	b M F Maharoof	0	1	0	0
N J O'Brien	c K C Sangakkara	b M Muralitharan	4	28	0	0
K J O'Brien	c S T Jayasuriya	b M Muralitharan	2	4	0	0
K E D Carroll		b M Muralitharan	0	2	0	0
D T Johnston	run out		0	4	0	0
W K McCallan	lbw	b M Muralitharan	0	9	0	0
D Langford-Smith	lbw	b W P U J C Vaas	18	21	2	1
W B Rankin	not out		7	17	1	0
Extras		2nb 2w 5lb	9			
Total		all out	77	(27.4 ovs)		

Bowler	O	M	R	W
W P U J C Vaas	5.4	1	18	1
K M D N Kulasekara	7.0	3	10	0
M F Maharoof	10.0	3	25	4
M Muralitharan	5.0	0	19	4

Fall of wicket			
28	J P Bray	49	D T Johnston
28	A C Botha	49	K J O'Brien
28	E J G Morgan	54	W K McCallan
46	W T S Porterfield	77	D Langford-Smith
48	N J O'Brien		
48	K E D Carroll		

Sri Lanka innings			runs	balls	4s	6s
W U Tharanga	c W T S Porterfield	b W B Rankin	0	7	0	0
S T Jayasuriya	not out		24	20	3	1
K C Sangakkara	c K E D Carroll	b D Langford-Smith	10	9	1	0
D P M D Jayawardene	not out		39	27	6	1
Extras		3nb 5w	8			
Total		for 2	81	(10.0 ovs)		

Bowler	O	M	R	W
W B Rankin	4.0	0	36	1
D Langford-Smith	3.0	0	29	1
A C Botha	1.0	0	4	0
K J O'Brien	1.0	0	4	0
K E D Carroll	1.0	0	8	0

Fall of wicket	
1	W U Tharanga
25	K C Sangakkara

Adrian Birrell with Paul Mooney, Kyle McCallan, Andrew White and Peter Gillespie, the four players who were there for his first and last game in charge of Ireland

16   Adrian Birrell

When Adrian Birrell took over as Ireland coach in March 2002, Irish cricket was at an all-time low. The season was about to start, and there was no coach of the national team in place. This followed a dismal ICC Trophy in Canada the previous summer, where Ireland did not even come close to gaining one of the three World Cup places which were on offer. Namibia, the Netherlands and Canada qualified for the 2003 tournament in South Africa, with Ireland finishing sixth out of seven teams in the table, below Scotland, the United Arab Emirates and the mighty United States of America, and staying ahead of Denmark only on run rate. The tournament ended Ken Rutherford's reign as Ireland coach, the former New Zealand international informing the ICU that he didn't want his contract to be renewed. This left the ICU with no national coach until Birrell took up the position six months later.

Born in Grahamstown in the Eastern Cape of South Africa, the Port Elizabeth native played first-class cricket for Eastern Province as an opening batsman and a left-arm spinner. He coached in the townships of Port Elizabeth for ten years – Birrell speaks the local language, Xhosa, fluently – before taking over his former club, Eastern Province, where he coached for three years. Birrell came into the Ireland job as a relative unknown, compared to the two previous high-profile coaches, Rutherford and former England international Mike Hendrick. The South African had a wealth of coaching experience, however, and this made him an ideal candidate for the position.

The Ireland job came about because of a family situation which found Birrell and his wife hundreds of miles apart. While Birrell coached at Eastern Province, his wife was working in East London as a partner for Deloitte & Touche. He saw an advertisement for the job and went for an interview knowing very little about Irish cricket, but the ICU recognised Birrell's experience, potential and enthusiasm, and decided that he was the man for the job.

ADRIAN BIRRELL:

I just went to an interview, not [knowing] very much at all [about Irish cricket]. It was a traumatic time for my wife and I. She was a partner with Deloitte's and had moved to East London. I was still living and working in Port Elizabeth, coaching Eastern Province for three years. The problems associated with living apart were among the main reasons for coming to Ireland. I was surprised at the number of clubs they had, and blown away by the passion and commitment of those involved in the game. The support from the Irish cricket family was phenomenal.

After the doomed World Cup qualifiers in Canada, Birrell's new team was barely inside the world's top twenty, and was languishing in the Second Division of the World Cricket League – the 2007 equivalent contains teams of the calibre of Oman, Uganda and Argentina. Birrell was either desperate or saw something in the Irish set-up that he felt he could work with. Considering that he was coaching at first-class level in South Africa, he could probably have held out for a job in English county cricket, so the decision to take the Ireland job was clearly not made out of desperation. The five short years that he spent with Ireland proved that the squad had potential and needed the right man to unlock it. It was obvious that Birrell was committed from the day he took the job.

ADRIAN BIRRELL:

I look forward to the challenges that lie ahead within Irish cricket. My objectives for the national side are to take it into Division One of the World League of non-Test playing countries as well as laying the foundations for entry into the 2007 World Cup. I am also keenly aware that the Irish sides at Under-13, Under-15, Under-17, and the women's senior team, are European champions, and I will see it as my responsibility to encourage the general growth of cricket throughout Ireland. I've been involved in cricket from the grass-roots level up, and setting up coaching structures within Eastern Province, and [the Irish position] looked like it was a similar challenge, where I could establish something through all levels of cricket, right from the national side down. And I would have some influence and input into the various levels. I enjoy that type of challenging work. I won't come in with any preconceived ideas. It will be negotiated, with everyone buying into the way forward... They [the players] are part of a decision-making process which determines the ground rules. It's getting everyone working in one direction, making sure everyone is goal-orientated to get Ireland towards the World Cup, and happy and motivated towards working towards the big picture.

At the time, Birrell's objectives were achievable but still quite ambitious for a new coach, who may have been putting unnecessary pressure on himself. But given the way Birrell works, and what he has achieved in the subsequent years, it was no surprise that all his objectives were met, and exceeded, in such a short space of time. Since Birrell took charge, Ireland have maintained their European titles at all age groups, now including the Under-19s and the senior team. He has also taken Ireland to victory in two InterContinental Cups, wins over the West Indies and Zimbabwe and, of course, easy qualification for the 2007 World Cup, when Ireland finished second behind Scotland at the 2005 ICC Trophy, held in Ireland, with the top five teams qualifying for the 2007 Cricket World Cup.

With almost two years to prepare for the World Cup, Birrell wasted no time in putting in place the team that he would bring to the Caribbean. First of all was a change of captain. After a loss of form at the end of the 2005 season, Jason Mollins was dropped from the international team. Trent Johnston was named as the new skipper, and Birrell spent 2006 assessing the players at his disposal, and building his squad around his Aussie-born leader. In August 2006, feeling confident that he had assembled the most consistent players from the past two years, Birrell named the fifteen that he would take to the World Cup. It was a shrewd move: he knew that the additional time would allow the players to focus on the tournament and to get to know their fellow squad members intimately before the trip to the Caribbean. There was no place for the out-of-form Mollins, which must have been a bitter pill for the former captain to swallow, considering that he had been captain when Ireland qualified for the Caribbean tournament.

ADRIAN BIRRELL:

I dropped the old captain, Jason Mollins, and made Trent [Johnston] skipper. Mollins hadn't scored consistently for two years but was also a victim of the squad's success: Trent, leading with passion and heart, won the Inter-continental Cup, beating Kenya in Namibia and then winning the European Championships. The team had gelled like never before. A successful team is very hard to change, and Jason was a victim of this.

Upon meeting Birrell, you could not but be carried along by the enthusiasm and belief that he exuded regarding the Ireland team and their capabilities going into the World Cup. He instilled his philosophy into the team, backing his players and emphasising the importance of the three disciplines of cricket (batting, bowling and fielding) – an approach which is particularly relevant to the one-day game. Birrell wanted all of his players to excel in at least two of the three disciplines. He recognised the importance of fielding in the one-day game: an outstanding performance by an individual in the field could save up to thirty runs in an innings, and this could be the difference between beating one of the bigger teams and being beaten by them. Players like William Porterfield cemented their place in the team with their fielding exploits, and while Kenny Carroll's inclusion in the squad was mainly down to the fact that he was batting superbly, it also helped that he could turn his arm over as a left-arm-Chinaman bowler, as well as being excellent in the field.

WILLIAM PORTERFIELD:

When Adrian Birrell took over, he told me that he wanted me to be the best fielder in Ireland, and it's something that I have worked very hard on. I need to perform in two disciplines, and because I don't bowl, I have to be strong in the field. And it's great when you hear people saying that we are one of the best fielding sides at the World Cup, because it's a reward for all the hard work we put in at training.

Porterfield's performances at point, Trent Johnston's at mid-on, and André Botha's and Eoin Morgan's in the slips, as well as the athleticism of some of the outfielders, proved that Ireland were well disciplined, and earned rave reviews from every cricket commentator at the tournament. And the team spirit that Birrell instilled in the squad went a long way towards getting these players to play for each other, for their country and for the coach. This was obvious from watching the team play and talking to the players about the coach.

ANDREW WHITE:

A lot of the credit [for Ireland's recent success] has to go to Adrian Birrell. He's been a great man-manager and a great motivator. He's put a squad together that is playing for him, and when you're playing for a man that has the respect of all the players, there's no doubt that a good team spirit is going to be there. It's been a unique experience being away for so long with the same group of lads, as we're used to being away for a weekend, so to be still going strong at the end of it all is a great sign for the future. If the nucleus of the squad stays together and the team spirit remains, we can go on to bigger and better things.

Taking the Irish squad to South Africa for three weeks before the World Cup was a risk that paid off for Birrell. He was keen to show the players where he was from and to introduce them to his family and friends, and to the place that he called home, Port Elizabeth. As the team was looking at three months on the road, after never having toured together for any substantial period before, Birrell's experiment could easily have gone wrong – with a potentially disastrous effect on Ireland's World Cup campaign. As it turned out, the trip was a great success, and while the results in Kenya didn't go to plan, the team spirit was alive for all to see in the Caribbean, with Birrell's side enjoying every game, whether they were beating one of the best teams in the world or taking a hammering from the world champions.

The team's performance at the World cup was testimony to the coach and to the five years of hard graft he had put in, studying, analysing and improving every aspect of Irish cricket. And Birrell was happy to work with people whom others may have deemed to pose a threat to his authority. He brought Mike Hendrick, the former coach, back in to work with his bowlers in the build-up to the World Cup, and invited Phil Simmons, his successor, to come and help with the coaching in the Caribbean.

Grabbing a last-gasp tie with Zimbabwe ensured that Ireland had achieved something significant at the World Cup. What happened next – the defeat of Pakistan and the qualification for the Super Eights – shocked the world and earned Birrell and his team legendary status in the annals of Irish cricketing history. But with qualification for the second phase came a host of new problems, both logistical and personal. Most of the team had to negotiate extra time off work; even Birrell had assumed that he would have been bowing out as Ireland coach after the West Indies game, and then, happily, had to commit to another four weeks working for the ICU.

ADRIAN BIRRELL:

It's a dream come true for me. I had planned a holiday in Mexico. I had to cancel that after we got to the Super Eights. I told the boys that by getting through to this stage, they have given me the greatest present ever. There is a great deal of satisfaction and a sense of accomplishment. This is the result of the hard work of five years. I am very proud of the boys.

KYLE McCALLAN:

I think it shows the distance that we've come over the last five years under Adi Birrell's reign. You know, I think when he took over we were playing Denmark at Malahide in front of two men and a dog. I think that [the Ireland team's recent achievements are] testament to the hard work that has been done over the last five years, and it's been special.

TRENT JOHNSTON:

Without a shadow of a doubt, Adi has been the best coach that I have ever played for. From a coaching aspect, he is the best mentor and friend that anyone could ever ask for. He's tough but he's fair and he's honest, and the way he approaches a game is phenomenal, it's what has turned Irish cricket around. And I've seen Irish cricket change since my first season in 1995 to now, we're now European champions at every level, and that's never been done before, so it's special to be part of this era of Irish cricket.

PETER GILLESPIE:

It's hard to put it into words, but he has brought us to another level altogether. The previous coaches brought us so far, but we still had a long way to go, and Adi took the steps required to get us to that level. Adi quickly identified that we were amateurs, but asked us to play and train like professionals. He made the hard slog worth while, as he always believed in us and always gave us confidence. Adi broke down the one-day game into its simplest [form] and he showed us how to play it. He identified everybody's role in the team and let you know what your role was in the team and how you were going to fit into the overall picture. And from there we got a basic plan in order and we just practised it and practised it and executed it. And the more we executed it, the more belief we had in ourselves, which has culminated in this World Cup, and anyone who has been following our progress over the past few years will tell you that it's no fluke, as we've worked so hard and deserve the success. It is all down to Adi and his tactics and the team he has around him. Adi is an emotional guy and wears his heart on his sleeve, and he gets very attached to players, and as a result, it makes it hard for him to leave out players that he likes. But he always puts the job first and always gets the best eleven players out on the pitch.

The four weeks of the Super Eights, where Ireland played six games in a short period of time against world-class opposition, took its toll on the players and Birrell, and this was evident during the last days of the tournament. There was a possibility that Ireland would go through the entire Super Eights without a victory, but thankfully an accomplished performance against Bangladesh saw Birrell get the victory that rekindled the spirit of Sabina Park. It was a great exhibition, with the team performing in every discipline, and beating another Test nation by playing the game the Adrian Birrell way. The coach looked exhausted as he faced the media after bowing out of Irish cricket against Sri Lanka. But now it was time to reflect, not only on the day's game or the past six weeks in the Caribbean, but also on his five years in charge of Irish cricket.

ADRIAN BIRRELL:

When I took over, we were probably ranked eighteenth or twentieth in the world. Now we're arguably the strongest Associate [nation]. And along the way, we've picked up some major scalps. Our fielding is excellent, we have a long batting line-up, and the bowling is very good when we get it right. But if you ask me what our greatest strength is, it's the team spirit. I am very proud of what we've achieved. It is not only me: we've got a great squad of players, we're very tight, there is a wonderful team spirit. Five years ago, we were ranked below Denmark, and now we're ranked ahead of the other Associate countries. It is a very satisfying moment for me to know I have moved it forward that much. It has been a great experience for me; the people have accepted me as one of their own. There have been hard decisions and tough times along the way, but the overriding feeling was that we made progress every year. We constantly moved it forward, and certainly so over the last few weeks

So what now for Adrian Birrell? The coach stepped down after the World Cup and made his last official appearance as Irish coach on *The Late Late Show* the week after returning from the Caribbean.

ADRIAN BIRRELL:

I plan to stay in Ireland and rest for a while. It's time I supported my wife and family. I hope to be involved with cricket in other ways, perhaps as a coach educator at an academy or in some sort of consultant role. I'll also look at motivational speaking. Either way, it will be something that doesn't take me away from home for too long. And I'm going to play a lot of golf.

Trent and Adi plan their World Cup strategy at the Amakhala Game Reserve in the Greater Addo and Frontier Country area of the Eastern Cape Province of South Africa, near Port Elizabeth

Adrian Birrell consults with assistant coach, Matt Dwyer and coach in waiting Phil Simmons in the nets at a training session

17   Looking Back and Forward

When people look back at the 2007 Cricket World Cup in the West Indies, they will remember several outstanding aspects of the competition: Ricky Ponting's Australia winning the trophy for the third time in a row – and winning every game en route to the final in Barbados; the batting of Matthew Hayden, who was the top scorer in the tournament, with 659 runs; Glenn McGrath bowing out of international cricket on a high as the tournament's leading wicket-taker, with twenty-six dismissals, and having overtaken Wasim Akram as the leading wicket-taker in World Cup history. And not forgetting Lasith Malinga's four wickets from four consecutive balls against South Africa, or Herschelle Gibbs' six sixes in one over – Dan van Bunge the unfortunate Netherlands bowler who will be forever remembered throughout the cricket world as a pub-quiz answer.

The memories of the Ireland team, the results, the players' attitude, and the two-thousand-strong Blarney Army will be right up there with the tournament highlights. Ireland tied their first-ever World Cup game with Zimbabwe, they beat Pakistan, to send the number-four-ranked team in the world crashing out of the tournament, and went on to record a historic win in the Super Eights against Bangladesh, to cement their place in the 2007 World Cup almanac. Adrian Birrell's team of amateurs, led by the inspirational Trent Johnston, played every game with smiles on their faces, and made friends wherever they went on their extended excursion in the Caribbean.

From a personal point of view, the moment that stands out was the finish to the Zimbabwe game. It was far from the team's greatest achievement at the tournament, but in terms of sheer sporting excitement, it wasn't topped. The win against Pakistan was a gradual thing, while the Bangladesh victory was virtually guaranteed almost an hour before the game finished. The last two overs of the Zimbabwe game hit every emotion associated with a live stadium sports experience. And just travelling amongst this great Irish squad and watching them achieve everything they have was also an experience that will take a lot of beating.

ANDREW WHITE:

It is very difficult to narrow it down to one. I think the whole Pakistan occasion caused everyone's emotions to soar high and low that day, a bit like the Zimbabwe game before it. I suppose for me being personally involved in that last over of the game against Zimbabwe in Ireland's first-ever World Cup game will always remain at the forefront of my mind, and it was an important tie. We had done so well in the game, Jeremy [Bray] had batted really well, hitting a hundred, and we were out of the game for a long time, but the bowlers did well to get us back into it, and although I bowled the last over, there was so much work done beforehand. Those two games will never be forgotten by any Irish supporter that watched the games.

TRENT JOHNSTON:

Meeting the President before coming out to the Caribbean was a highlight. Not many people get to meet her, so to sit down and have afternoon tea with her was very special. Getting off the bus in Ocho Rios after beating Pakistan, where it took me forty-five minutes to walk into the hotel lobby, was amazing, just chatting to everyone and being congratulated let you know that you were part of something special, and to have my parents and my wife and kids over made it even more amazing; it is something that will stay with me forever. But to achieve what we have achieved over here, qualifying for the Super Eights and being competitive in all but two games, is remarkable. There's been lots of team highlights as well, the nail-biter against Zimbabwe, and then to beat Pakistan and turn it around against Bangladesh after the Australia game, when most of our team only play club cricket, not even first-class cricket, is a massive achievement for every one of the guys.

ANDRÉ BOTHA:

I think the Bangladesh games was one of the best games we've ever played, so that's something that will stick with me forever. That was my highlight of the trip.

JEREMY BRAY:

Getting to play against all the best cricketers in the world in the space of five or six weeks was a fantastic experience. We don't get to play too many big games playing for Ireland, so rubbing shoulders with the world's greats was unbelievable, you can't describe it.

PHIL SIMMONS:

At the end of the day, it's one big highlight, as no one expected the lads to do anything. The wins against Pakistan and Bangladesh stand out, but they have learned so much from the whole experience. And they have the experience now, and with lots of guys in their early twenties already carrying the team, the future is very bright for Irish cricket.

ALBERT KIRK (cameraman):

The highlight of the trip was obviously the Pakistan match. It was one of the best sporting moments that I have ever seen – and I've seen a lot. I've even seen Northern Ireland beat England, but that was right up there.

PAUL KEOGH (cameraman):

On the pitch, my highlight was Ireland's fielding performance against Pakistan, which bordered on perfection – all ten Pakistani batsmen were caught out. Off the field, earlier the same day, some bloke dressed as St Patrick leading the Irish fans into Sabina Park... and having his staff confiscated by security staff at the stadium entrance.

ADRIAN BIRRELL:

The game againt Pakistan was the highlight. Getting into the World Cup was truly amazing, and that was the highlight. I stuck to the principles and philosphies that I have learned over the last twenty years, and I got my rewards.

BOYD RANKIN:

Getting Ed Joyce first ball and getting [Michael] Vaughan as well in that first spell was amazing. It was great to be playing against the best players in the world and the players you watch on the television.

NEIL BRITTAIN (UTV):

The highlight of my trip was a toss-up between the Pakistan game and the celebrations that came after it in Ocho Rios. It was probably the game itself, as we beat one of the superpowers of world cricket, and you had to rub your eyes and check that you were actually believing what you were seeing.

KENNY CARROLL:

My personal higlight was getting the catch in the Sri Lanka game, catching [Kumar] Sangakkara. The team highlight has to be the Pakistan match on St Paddy's Day in Jamaica.

JERRY O'SULLIVAN (NewsTalk):

There were so many highlights that it is hard to concentrate on just one. But my favourite was winning against Pakistan. At one stage the Irish fans were having so much fun doing a conga line, and after a couple of Pakistan players, I think Youssuf and Inzamam, were bowled out for only a few runs, the Irish fans started singing 'Are you England in disguise?'. The fact that the Irish fans were in a position to sing something as sarcastic as that to one of the best teams in the world was a real highlight for me. I'll never forget it.

RICHARD GILLIS (the *Irish Times*):

There were lots of highlights – the Pakistan game, the celebrations in Ocho Rios – but I've really got a soft spot for the Zimbabwe game. That's where it all started, getting the tie, Bray's century. That was a turning point, as we wouldn't have qualified if it wasn't for that.

ROBBIE IRWIN (RTÉ):

To perfectly honest, I never thought we were going to go in the first place, so that was a highlight. Then playing Zimbabwe, and it was like in soccer, as if we were 4–0 down with five minutes to go and we got a 4–4 draw. And then we go and beat the Pakistan team and then everything that went with it; it was like an Agatha Christie story. When you put the whole thing together, it was a journey, an adventure, and it was a work experience that I'll never ever forget.

IAIN KNOX:

In Trinidad, myself and Matt Dwyer went out with a guy, just for a drive around the city, and ended up in Brian Lara's house, having a beer at his bar in his living room. It was surreal. He had his BBC Foreign Sports Personality award sitting on the bar, and none of the guys were there, and we knew that they would be gutted when they heard the story. But on every island there was a story. But for me that stands out, and all the touristy things we've done, which were all brilliant, and the way we've been escorted around the place with police escorts, that's just a story in itself every day.

NIALL O'BRIEN:

It was great to be in Jamaica, the home of Bob Marley, and just to get the chance to come up against some of the greatest players and to get to chat to the likes of Brian Lara. I really enjoyed playing against the best teams and the best players in the world. And it's nice to be able to face the best bowlers in the world on such a big stage and test your skills against the best and come out on top.

KEVIN O'BRIEN:

The World Cup has been the greatest experience I have ever had in my cricketing career. It's been a great learning curve, as every day you learn something new playing against the best players in the world. And it's always great batting with Niall, and I was really happy with the way I batted against Bangladesh and New Zealand, they were two really good knocks. Everywhere we've gone has been a new experience, right from the time we went to Adi's place in South Africa – we had some fun there – and then got into the cricketing side of it in Port Elizabeth town. Then we had a disappointing time in Kenya, but after that we had a great week in Abu Dhabi and qualified for the ICC final. And then these six weeks in the Caribbean have been beyond belief really.

PETER GILLESPIE:

There have been so many highlights throughout my Ireland cricket career, both personal and team highlights, but the victory over Pakistan in the World Cup at Sabina Park surpassed everything. The atmosphere, St Patrick's Day, people coming from all over the world, it just made that one day better than any other. My favourite place was Barbados. A group of us from Strabane go on tour there every couple of years. And you can't beat the island – the beaches – and the newly developed stadium is fantastic, so to get a win there was really special.

KYLE McCALLAN:

Quite simply, the team highlight has to be Sabina Park on St Patrick's Day, beating Pakistan, closely followed by the win against Bangladesh, that showed the sort of character and backbone that this side has. The stadiums have been fabulous and the crowds have been great, but the whole experience is something that I'll take with me until my dying day. We're savouring every last minute of it. Over the past six weeks, we've created thousands of memories. I believe that there are books being written and videos being made, and I'll look forward with a huge amount of pride to watching and reading these in the coming months and really just seeing what we experienced, because when you're living it day to day, sometimes you're living in a little cocoon, and you're missing out on what's going on. And then I'll realise just how special it has been.

The Irish have time for one last squad photo before they bow out of the 2007 Cricket World Cup

The Ireland experience was definitely one of the positives of what will inevitably go down as a poor World Cup. Pakistan coach Bob Woolmer's death turned into a badly handled – and mistaken – murder investigation, and the tournament also went horribly wrong as a corporate exercise, with ticket prices, sponsors, brands and logos becoming more important than the one ingredient that is a constant at any successful sporting event – the fans. Even the World Cup final ended in farce, with Australia having to bowl their final overs against Sri Lanka in virtual darkness.

JOHN KENNY (RTÉ):

I had the delight of commentating on the prestigious Test Match Special radio show for the BBC during Ireland's matches at the World Cup. I was only due to work for the Zimbabwe game in Jamaica, but when England's game on St Patrick's day ended early, BBC Radio 5Live went to Sabina Park for the last two hours of the Pakistan game where I was asked to commentate with Alison Mitchell for Ireland's famous win, which was a great pleasure. And by the time the Ireland squad got to Guyana, BBC's Test Match Special decided to commentate on all of Ireland's remaining games, which meant that I became an integral part of their team. For me, being part of the institution that is TMS at the World Cup will live long in the memory.

When the World Cup was awarded to the West Indies, the cricketing community got very excited about the prospect of thronged stadia, jam-packed with the most passionate, colourful and entertaining supporters in the world. As things turned out, barely a game was sold out before the semi-final stage, and all noise-making instruments – bugles, conches, drums and horns – were banned, as were picnic baskets, and even bottled water at one stage. (You could buy the sponsor's water inside the stadium). The locals were priced out of the ticket market and, as a result, stayed away, with the opening game, West Indies against Pakistan in Jamaica being the closest thing to a full house in the group stages.

Before the World Cup, most Irish people wouldn't have known that Ireland even had a cricket team. But from now on, cricket in Ireland will be placed into two categories: Before *and After* Cricket World Cup 2007. But how will Irish cricket build on the team's successes at the World Cup and turn the game into one of the major sports in the country?

The team arrived back in Ireland a week after their final game against Sri Lanka, and immediately had to adapt to a new coach, Phil Simmons, and prepare for their first competitive game of the (already started) season – a Friends Provident clash against English county cricket side Kent, less than a week after touching down at Dublin Airport. At least Simmons had spent most of the World Cup campaign amongst the team and was already familiar with the players he would have to work with. But Paul Mooney had retired, and Eoin Morgan, Boyd Rankin and Niall O'Brien were back at their clubs in England. This left only the bare bones of a squad for the first game, to be played in Belfast the following Sunday.

The Kent game was a low-key event: despite the fact that the sun was shining and the Irish heroes were back on home soil for the first time since their World Cup exploits, a paltry crowd turned up to Stormont, and it was business as usual for an Ireland fixture. The rest of the tournament provided very little to cheer about from an Irish point of view: the side failed to win any of the nine games against English county opposition. Ed Joyce and Eoin Morgan helping Middlesex to victory in one of the games was a particularly bitter pill for the Irish team to swallow. It didn't help matters when more of the World Cup squad pulled out: John Mooney made himself unavailable due to work commitments, Peter Gillespie retired, and Jeremy Bray took a stand against the ICU, saying that he was no longer available for selection as he was unhappy with the way affairs had been handled since the squad's return from the Caribbean. The two professionals that Ireland employed for these games didn't work out either: South African Nantie Hayward failed to impress, and New Zealander Jesse Ryder made more of an impact off the field than than on it, allegedly missing a flight, which led to a no-show for the Surrey game at the Oval.

It turned out that the World Cup squad hadn't received all the money that was due to them from their Caribbean adventure, and things came to a head when the players decided that they would not talk to the media until matters were resolved. ICU finances were due to be bolstered by the arrival of South Africa and India for a one-day-international series at Stormont, but the games, which included an Ireland international against both nations, coincided with some of the most inclement weather witnessed in an Irish summer in recent years, and only a couple of hundred people braved the elements at a rain-interrupted series at the Belfast venue. The West Indies drew a sizeable crowd to Clontarf, but again the weather wreaked havoc, and this, coupled with the visitors' reluctance to play in tricky conditions, resulted in the match being abandoned. At least the squad had by this stage received what was owed to them, and relations between players and officials got back to normal.

With so many of the World Cup squad missing, the new coach's tenure was as tough as they come: he had to rely on others to recommend players for him to call up, without knowing too much about them. Alex Cusack from Clontarf impressed with bat and ball and won the man of the match accolade against South Africa, and Greg Thompson broke back into the squad in impressive fashion, the right-arm leg-spinner picking up wickets against Scotland and Bermuda in the InterContinental Cup.

The season ended in August with a comprehensive victory for Ireland against Bermuda in Clontarf. The Irish won with an innings and a day to spare, proving that they were at a different level from many of their Associate counterparts. The previous game with Scotland had ended in a tie. Ireland and Scotland are currently in a kind of limbo – below the Test nations but head and shoulders above the other Associate nations, especially in the longer form of the game.

So what's next for the Ireland team and for Irish cricket in general? A professional structure had long been in the pipeline, but the success in the West Indies seemed to bring it to the top of the agenda, putting immediate pressure on the new ICU CEO, Warren Deutrom. The Irish game needs to stop losing its best players to the English county scene, and has to reward its best players with professional, or at least semi-professional, contracts, to show players that they are appreciated and to ensure that the coach has access to his squad throughout the year and not just the night before a game. Participation in the Friends Provident Trophy may not be a long-term staple on the Irish cricket calendar unless the Ireland team is awarded first-class-county status. More likely, the Ireland team will play a great deal of their season throughout the Irish autumn and winter in foreign climes, whether against fellow Associate sides or, preferably, in arranged series against the weaker of the Test nations, such as Zimbabwe and Bangladesh. There is talk of a pre-season trip back to the Caribbean in 2008, by which time, hopefully, the ICU and the players will all be singing from the same hymn-sheet and Irish cricket will be able to make the strides forward that the weather, red tape, the extended season, and the pressure of the World Cup prevented it from making in the summer of 2007.

While the 2007 Cricket World Cup was not an outstanding affair for the purists, it will always be remembered very fondly by everyone involved in Irish cricket. It was Ireland's first appearance at the event, so they have nothing to compare it to. But one thing is for certain: all future appearances – of which there should be many – will forever be compared to the Caribbean experience of 2007.

EMMET RIORDAN (*IRISH INDEPENDENT*):

In an era when our sports stars move further and further away from their supporters, one of the highlights of Ireland's participation at the World Cup was the shared sense of achievement between the players and the fans. The reception given to the team after the stunning victory over Pakistan on St Patrick's Day, and their willingness to share it with those who travelled to Jamaica, will live long in the memory.

Ireland Statistics

BATTING   Runs scored

Player	Mat	Inns	NO	Runs	HS	Ave	SR	100	50	0	4s	6s
NJ O'Brien	9	9	0	216	72	24.00	57.75	0	2	1	17	1
JP Bray	9	9	1	212	115*	26.50	62.72	1	0	2	22	2
WTS Porterfield	9	9	0	172	85	19.11	45.38	0	1	2	7	0
KJ O'Brien	8	8	1	170	49	24.28	64.63	0	0	0	13	5
DT Johnston	8	8	2	129	30	21.50	89.58	0	0	1	8	5
AR White	8	8	0	128	38	16.00	73.98	0	0	1	13	0
EJG Morgan	9	9	0	91	28t	10.11	50.83	0	0	2	11	1
D Langford-Smith	9	8	4	67	18	16.75	93.05	0	0	0	6	2
AC Botha	7	7	1	62	28	10.33	47.32	0	0	2	2	1
WK McCallan	9	8	1	33	20*	4.71	44.00	0	0	4	2	0
JF Mooney	2	2	0	23	23	11.50	51.11	0	0	1	2	0
WB Rankin	9	4	3	15	7*	15.00	33.33	0	0	1	1	0
PG Gillespie	1	1	0	2	2	2.00	25.00	0	0	0	0	0
KED Carroll	1	1	0	0	0	0.00	0.00	0	0	1	0	0
PJK Mooney	1	1	0	0	0	0.00	0.00	0	0	1	0	0

BATTING   Top scores

Player	Runs	Balls	4s	6s	SR	Opposition	Ground	Date
JP Bray	115*	13/	10	2	83.94	v Zimbabwe	Kingston	15 Mar 2007
WTS Porterfield	85	136	3	0	62.50	v Bangladesh	Bridgetown	15 Apr 2007
NJ O'Brien	72	107	6	1	67.28	v Pakistan	Kingston	17 Mar 2007
NJ O'Brien	63	88	4	0	71.59	v England	Providence	30 Mar 2007
KJ O'Brien	49	45	2	3	108.88	v New Zealand	Providence	9 Apr 2007
KJ O'Brien	48	44	2	2	109.09	v Bangladesh	Bridgetown	15 Apr 2007
JP Bray	41	72	7	0	56.94	v West Indies	Kingston	23 Mar 2007
AR White	38	35	4	0	108.57	v England	Providence	30 Mar 2007
WTS Porterfield	31	68	1	0	45.58	v England	Providence	30 Mar 2007
JP Bray	31	70	1	0	44.28	v Bangladesh	Bridgetown	15 Apr 2007
AR White	30	30	5	0	100.00	v South Africa	Providence	3 Apr 2007
NJ O'Brien	30	75	2	0	40.00	v New Zealand	Providence	9 Apr 2007
DT Johnston	30	23	2	1	130.43	v Bangladesh	Bridgetown	15 Apr 2007
AR White	28	48	3	0	58.33	v Zimbabwe	Kingston	15 Mar 2007
AC Botha	28	56	1	1	50.00	v West Indies	Kingston	23 Mar 2007
EJG Morgan	28	50	4	0	56.00	v South Africa	Providence	3 Apr 2007
DT Johnston	27	21	1	2	128.57	v England	Providence	30 Mar 2007
NJ O'Brien	25	37	3	0	67.56	v South Africa	Providence	3 Apr 2007
JF Mooney	23	44	2	0	52.27	v Australia	Bridgetown	13 Apr 2007
EJG Morgan	21	27	4	0	77.77	v Zimbabwe	Kingston	15 Mar 2007
WK McCallan	20*	24	2	0	83.33	v West Indies	Kingston	23 Mar 2007
DT Johnston	20	24	2	0	83.33	v Zimbabwe	Kingston	15 Mar 2007
JP Bray	20	29	4	0	68.96	v Sri Lanka	St George's	18 Apr 2007

BATTING   Highest partnerships

Partners	Runs	Wkt	Opposition	Ground	Match Date
WTS Porterfield, JP Bray	92	1st	v Bangladesh	Bridgetown	15 Apr 2007
NJ O'Brien, KJ O'Brien	75	4th	v New Zealand	Providence	9 Apr 2007
WTS Porterfield, NJ O'Brien	61	3rd	v England	Providence	30 Mar 2007
JP Bray, EJG Morgan	58	2nd	v West Indies	Kingston	23 Mar 2007
DT Johnston, AR White	58	7th	v England	Providence	30 Mar 2007
JP Bray, AR White	56	6th	v Zimbabwe	Kingston	15 Mar 2007
WTS Porterfield, KJ O'Brien	48	4th	v Bangladesh	Bridgetown	15 Apr 2007
WTS Porterfield, NJ O'Brien	47	3rd	v Pakistan	Kingston	17 Mar 2007
AC Botha, KJ O'Brien	47	5th	v West Indies	Kingston	23 Mar 2007
NJ O'Brien, AC Botha	44	4th	v England	Providence	30 Mar 2007
JP Bray, EJG Morgan	43	2nd	v Zimbabwe	Kingston	15 Mar 2007
JP Bray, D Langford-Smith	39	9th	v Zimbabwe	Kingston	15 Mar 2007
AR White, AC Botha	39	5th	v South Africa	Providence	3 Apr 2007
KJ O'Brien, DT Johnston	39	5th	v Bangladesh	Bridgetown	15 Apr 2007
NJ O'Brien, KJ O'Brien	38	5th	v Pakistan	Kingston	17 Mar 2007

BOWLING   Wickets

Player	Mat	Overs	Mdns	Runs	Wkts	Best	Ave	Econ	SR
WB Rankin	9	59.2	4	324	12	3/32	27.00	5.46	29.6
WK McCallan	9	58.4	3	233	10	2/12	23.30	3.97	35.2
DT Johnston	8	50.2	3	258	8	2/40	32.25	5.12	37.7
D Langford-Smith	9	66.0	4	291	7	2/27	41.57	4.40	56.5
AC Botha	7	49.0	7	181	5	2/5	36.20	3.69	58.8
AR White	8	18.1	1	89	3	2/45	29.66	4.89	36.3
KJ O'Brien	8	18.0	1	100	3	1/8	33.33	5.55	36.0
KED Carroll	1	1.0	0	8	0	-	-	8.00	-
JF Mooney	2	5.0	1	36	0	-	-	7.20	-
PJK Mooney	1	3.3	0	40	0	-	-	11.42	-

Tournament Statistics

BATTING   Runs scored

Player	Mat	Inns	NO	Runs	HS	Ave	SR	100	50	0	4s	6s
1 ML Hayden (Aus)	11	10	1	659	158	73.22	101.07	3	1	0	69	18
2 DPMD Jayawardene (SL)	11	11	2	548	115*	60.88	85.09	1	4	0	40	10
3 RT Ponting (Aus)	11	9	1	539	113	67.37	95.39	1	4	0	53	11
4 SB Styris (NZ)	10	9	3	499	111*	83.16	83.44	1	4	0	45	6
5 JH Kallis (SA)	10	9	3	485	128*	80.83	83.91	1	3	0	43	7
6 ST Jayasuriya (SL)	11	11	1	467	115	46.70	98.31	2	2	0	47	14
7 AC Gilchrist (Aus)	11	11	1	453	149	45.30	103.89	1	2	0	58	10
8 KP Pietersen (Eng)	9	9	1	444	104	55.50	81.02	2	3	0	36	5
9 GC Smith (SA)	10	10	1	443	91	49.22	104.48	0	5	0	55	6
10 MJ Clarke (Aus)	11	9	4	436	93*	87.20	94.98	0	4	0	40	7
27 NJ O'Brien (Ire)	9	9	0	216	72	24.00	57.75	0	2	1	17	1
28 JP Bray (Ire)	9	9	1	212	115*	26.50	62.72	1	0	2	22	2

BATTING   Highest scores

Player	Runs	Balls	4s	6s	SR	Team	Opposition	Ground	Match Date
Imran Nazir	160	121	14	8	132.23	Pakistan	v Zimbabwe	Kingston	21 Mar 2007
ML Hayden	158	143	14	4	110.48	Australia	v West Indies	North Sound	27 Mar 2007
AC Gilchrist	149	104	13	8	143.26	Australia	v Sri Lanka	Bridgetown	28 Apr 2007
AB de Villiers	146	130	12	5	112.30	South Africa	v West Indies	St George's	10 Apr 2007
JH Kallis	128*	109	11	5	117.43	South Africa	v Netherlands	Basseterre	16 Mar 2007
BJ Hodge	123	89	8	7	138.20	Australia	v Netherlands	Basseterre	18 Mar 2007
JP Bray	115*	137	10	2	83.94	Ireland	v Zimbabwe	Kingston	15 Mar 2007
DPMD Jayawardene	115*	109	10	3	105.50	Sri Lanka	v New Zealand	Kingston	24 Apr 2007
ST Jayasuriya	115	101	10	4	113.86	Sri Lanka	v West Indies	Providence	1 Apr 2007
V Sehwag	114	87	17	3	131.03	India	v Bermuda	Port of Spain	19 Mar 2007

BOWLING   Most wickets

Player	Mat	Overs	Mdns	Runs	Wkts	Best	Ave	Econ	SR	4	5
1 GD McGrath (Aus)	11	80.5	5	357	26	3/14	13.73	4.41	18.6	0	0
2 M Muralitharan (SL)	10	84.4	1	351	23	4/19	15.26	4.14	22.0	2	0
3 SW Tait (Aus)	11	84.3	1	467	23	4/39	20.30	5.52	22.0	1	0
4 GB Hogg (Aus)	11	82.5	6	332	21	4/27	15.80	4.00	23.6	2	0
5 SL Malinga (SL)	8	58.2	6	284	18	4/54	15.77	4.86	19.4	1	0
6 NW Bracken (Aus)	10	71.4	10	258	16	4/19	16.12	3.60	26.8	1	0
7 DL Vettori (NZ)	10	97.4	2	447	16	4/23	27.93	4.57	36.6	1	0
8 A Flintoff (Eng)	8	69.0	3	298	14	4/43	21.28	4.31	29.5	1	0
9 AJ Hall (SA)	9	76.0	5	335	14	5/18	23.92	4.40	32.5	0	1
10 CK Langeveldt (SA)	8	66.0	3	361	14	5/39	25.78	5.46	28.2	0	1
11 DBL Powell (WI)	9	85.0	9	385	14	3/38	27.50	4.52	36.4	0	0
17 WB Rankin (Ire)	9	59.2	4	324	12	3/32	27.00	5.46	29.6	0	0
19 WK McCallan (Ire)	9	58.4	3	233	10	2/12	23.30	3.97	35.2	0	0

BOWLING   Best economy rate *(Minimum of 200 balls)*

Player	Mat	Overs	Mdns	Runs	Wkts	Best	Ave	Econ	SR
1 SE Bond (NZ)	8	69.4	9	213	13	3/31	16.38	3.05	32.1
2 SM Pollock (SA)	10	84.0	10	296	8	2/17	37.00	3.52	63.0
3 NW Bracken (Aus)	10	71.4	10	258	16	4/19	16.12	3.60	26.8
4 WPUJC Vaas (SL)	10	77.4	15	286	13	3/33	22.00	3.68	35.8
5 AC Botha (Ire)	7	49.0	7	181	5	2/5	36.20	3.69	58.8
6 Syed Rasel (Ban)	7	62.0	7	239	8	2/25	29.87	3.85	46.5
7 WK McCallan (Ire)	9	58.4	3	233	10	2/12	23.30	3.97	35.2
8 GB Hogg (Aus)	11	82.5	6	332	21	4/27	15.80	4.00	23.6
9 JDP Oram (NZ)	9	62.3	7	252	10	3/23	25.20	4.03	37.5
10 M Muralitharan (SL)	10	84.4	1	351	23	4/19	15.26	4.14	22.0

BOWLING   Best strike rates

Player	Mat	Overs	Mdns	Runs	Wkts	Best	Ave	Econ	SR
1 GD McGrath (Aus)	11	80.5	5	357	26	3/14	13.73	4.41	18.6
2 SL Malinga (SL)	8	58.2	6	284	18	4/54	15.77	4.86	19.4
3 SW Tait (Aus)	11	84.3	1	467	23	4/39	20.30	5.52	22.0
4 M Muralitharan (SL)	10	84.4	1	351	23	4/19	15.26	4.14	22.0
5 GB Hogg (Aus)	11	82.5	6	332	21	4/27	15.80	4.00	23.6
6 A Nel (SA)	6	52.2	6	217	12	5/45	18.08	4.14	26.1
7 NW Bracken (Aus)	10	71.4	10	258	16	4/19	16.12	3.60	26.8
8 CK Langeveldt (SA)	8	66.0	3	361	14	5/39	25.78	5.46	28.2
9 MF Maharoof (SL)	6	44.0	5	198	9	4/23	22.00	4.50	29.3
10 A Flintoff (Eng)	8	69.0	3	298	14	4/43	21.28	4.31	29.5
11 WB Rankin (Ire)	9	59.2	4	324	12	3/32	27.00	5.46	29.6
16 WK McCallan (Ire)	9	58.4	3	233	10	2/12	23.30	3.97	35.2

BOWLING   Best economy bowling in an innings

Player	Overs	Mdns	Runs	Wkts	Econ	Team	Opposition	Ground	Match Date
1 AC Botha	8.0	4	5	2	0.62	Ireland	v Pakistan	Kingston	17 Mar 2007
2 SM Pollock	6.0	3	4	1	0.66	South Africa	v Netherlands	Basseterre	16 Mar 2007
3 KMDN Kulasekara	7.0	3	10	0	1.42	Sri Lanka	v Ireland	St George's	18 Apr 2007
4 SE Bond	10.0	4	15	2	1.50	New Zealand	v Bangladesh	North Sound	2 Apr 2007
5 WF Stelling	8.0	3	12	3	1.50	Netherlands	v Scotland	Basseterre	22 Mar 2007
6 GB Hogg	6.0	2	9	1	1.50	Australia	v Ireland	Bridgetown	13 Apr 2007
7 WPUJC Vaas	7.0	4	11	1	1.57	Sri Lanka	v Bangladesh	Port of Spain	21 Mar 2007
8 CD Collymore	7.0	1	11	2	1.57	West Indies	v Bangladesh	Bridgetown	19 Apr 2007
9 M Muralitharan	9.0	0	15	1	1.66	Sri Lanka	v Bangladesh	Port of Spain	21 Mar 2007
10 SM Pollock	10.0	2	17	0	1.70	South Africa	v England	Bridgetown	17 Apr 2007
20 WK McCallan	5.4	1	12	2	2.11	Ireland	v Pakistan	Kingston	17 Mar 2007

FIELDING   Most catches

Player	Mat	Inns	Ct	Max
PD Collingwood (Eng)	9	9	8	2
GC Smith (SA)	10	10	8	2
EJG Morgan (Ire)	9	9	7	3
HH Gibbs (SA)	10	10	7	2
ML Hayden (Aus)	11	11	7	2
RT Ponting (Aus)	11	11	7	2
Aftab Ahmed (Ban)	9	9	6	2
Tamim Iqbal (Ban)	9	9	6	2
LPC Silva (SL)	11	11	6	3
SO Tikolo (Kenya)	3	3	5	3
DT Johnston (Ire)	8	8	5	2
WTS Porterfield (Ire)	9	9	5	1

WICKETKEEPING   Most dismissals

Player	Mat	Inns	Dis	Ct	St	Max Dis Inns
AC Gilchrist (Aus)	11t	11	17	12	5	4 (4ct 0st)
KC Sangakkara (SL)	11	11	15	11	4	3 (3ct 0st)
BB McCullum (NZ)	10	10	14	13	1	4 (4ct 0st)
D Ramdin (WI)	9	9	13	13	0	4 (4ct 0st)
PA Nixon (Eng)	9	9	9	7	2	2 (2ct 0st)
NJ O'Brien (Ire)	9	9	9	9	0	2 (2ct 0st)
MV Boucher (SA)	10	10	9	9	0	2 (2ct 0st)
MS Dhoni (India)	3	3	7	5	2	3 (3ct 0st)
Kamran Akmal (Pak)	3	3	5	3	2	4 (3ct 1st)
BRM Taylor (Zim)	3	3	5	4	1	4 (3ct 1st)